I Am the Ocean

Samita Sarkar

Blossoms
BOOKS

The Bhagavad Gita quotes are taken from *The Bhagavad Gita As It Is*, as translated by A.C. Bhaktivedanta Swami Prabhupada. The text is freely available online at Vedabase.

I hope you enjoy my journey.

This book is dedicated to The Supreme Controller, my friend and well-wisher, Lord Krishna.

"...Of bodies of water I am the ocean."

—*The Bhagavad Gita*, 10.24

Table of Contents

Searching

In my early twenties, I was lost.

I had graduated cum laude from university and spent over a year looking for a job. I had no luck. To fill my days, I had taken to learning Spanish (through library books, YouTube videos, and a formerly amazing site called LiveMocha.com) and going for increasingly long runs so that I didn't die of boredom or depression. I was really just running from my problems, running away the stress. The longer I went without a job, the higher my stress levels became, and the more I ran.

Nothing that I had learned within the confines of my alma mater's ivory towers had truly prepared me for my life beyond. I always figured that I'd be snatched up by a firm as soon as I graduated. Why wouldn't I be? I was at the top of my class, and I was amazing at what I did.

But without classes to attend and assignments to work on, I found it difficult to gather the gumption to get out of bed in the morning. I just wanted to seamlessly transition from the strict schedule of student life to the strict and regimented schedule of a nine-to-fiver. Having no external source assigning me tasks to accomplish left me with a lack of direction. Slowly, I felt the girl who had graduated with so much self-esteem slipping away, giving rise to someone far less confident. I constantly asked myself, what was the purpose of it all?

I did everything I was supposed to do. I responded to job postings. I attended business networking events. I approached employment agencies. I made cold calls and sent cold emails. I reached out to strangers in my field on LinkedIn.

In the nine months I had spent diligently job hunting, some very strange things happened to me. I received interview requests that mysteriously ended up in my junk folder. Responses I did receive ended up being red herrings. I ran into car trouble on a major highway on my way to an interview. Resumes of mine were "lost," even when I had networked my application in through an internal connection. Most impressively, I once got caught in a major flood.

I really wanted God to give me a sign, and His message was loud and clear: office life was not for me. The question became, what was?

A Life Altering Decision

Stricken with anxiety in the scorching heat of July, I knew that to find out what I wanted from life, I needed to take some time away in order to deeply understand what kind of person I truly was. I was twenty-three years old.

I had a little bit of money saved from wetting my feet in freelance writing and editorial internships, so I decided to use it to take a trip. I was an only child who was raised frugally, and I seldom travelled during my childhood or youth (I was 26 when my parents and I took our first family vacation), so this was a big deal for me. I was my mother's daughter and thrifty to the core, but I knew that at that moment, I had to be selfish. I had to do something for myself, even if I ended up spending a bit of money.

What I didn't know was that the trip I was about to take would set the course for the rest of my life. It would be the first of many solo journeys, and was my first time being completely on my own. My entire life, I had been enveloped by the safety net of school, part-time jobs, family obligations, and friends. So for almost one month, I decided to be a gypsy. With no one to answer to but myself, and no company save for a small cloth journal, my favourite book, and a locket around my neck with a picture of The Divine Couple, I was ready to find out exactly who I was and what I was made of. How would I spend my days? How would I carry myself in various social situations? There was so much I didn't even realize about myself. What would I do when I had absolutely nothing *to* do?

I was ready to stop running, and embrace that cold terror. I hoped I would like my own company!

But despite my daydreams of far-away beaches on the African coast or the Indian Ocean, I was still essentially broke, meaning that any travel I did was limited to bussing distance. This ruled out anything foreign except for The States, which made my decision easy. Besides, I always loved the U.S. of A. I never spent much time there, and in Canada it was common to jokingly look down on our neighbours to the south, but I held nothing but warm feelings for them. After all, I had grown up reading American books, watching American movies, and listening to American music.

I consulted Google Maps. It definitely made the most sense to explore the East Coast. Not only would I get to see major metropolises like The Big Apple and the Nation's Capital, but I'd also get to explore the quiet beauty of the rural Deep South, and end my stay on a relaxing beach in southern Florida—where I'd finally have the chance to put my Spanish to good use.

On top of everything else, I'd get lots of chances to glimpse—perhaps even bathe in—the gorgeous, mysterious, awe-inspiring, seemingly endless ocean, an impersonal manifestation of God on Earth.

I started planning my trip. With forty dollars spent on an overnight bus trip, I could find myself in New York City. From there, it was only another ten bucks or so to get to Washington DC! The quaint, and famously haunted Savannah, Georgia seemed like a good spot for a third major stop, and if I made it all the way down to the country's southernmost city, Miami, I could get a crazy good deal on a flight back to Toronto. (Like I said, thrifty to the core.)

I took another look at the online map of all the cities that offered Megabus service: virtually everywhere in the eastern US. Some fares were as low as a dollar. I could go places I'd only read about in books, as well as places I'd never heard of at all. I felt sick to my stomach with the excitement.

Once I had planned my basic itinerary, there was still the issue of accommodation. I looked at booking websites in NYC: All hotels seemed to be priced at a minimum of a hundred bucks, with the cheapest of hostels (no Wi-Fi/no towels) adding up to fifty dollars after a ridiculous fifteen percent state tax.

I had to look into alternative methods of finding accommodation. I spent a lot of time on LiveMocha.com, an online community where people who wanted to learn different foreign languages could take free online classes and mark each other's assignments. There were a lot of South Americans on the site who wanted to learn English, and I edited their submissions. In turn, they edited my Spanish work. I had made many pen pals on the site. (Because all good things must come to an end, their competitor, the language-learning giant Rosetta Stone, eventually bought LiveMocha.com and ran this amazing resource with a thriving community into the ground.)

When I told a pen pal that I wanted to travel on a shoestring budget, he told me about Couchsurfing.org, another online community website. It was a place where travellers could go to network, offer/accept a couch or an empty room, and find travel companions for road trips.

It sounded pretty risky, but it was also a great idea.

*

I bit the bullet and made a Couchsurfing.org account. I filled out my profile:

ABOUT ME:

When I go to a new country, I want to know everything about it. I want to know where all the major cities are and how to get around. I want to speak the language fluently, see all the historical sites/museums/temples, national parks, beaches. (I know that this is not usually realistic.)

Now that that was done, I began to browse through the users located in New York.

Profile #1:

I saw an elderly woman with a kind face.

5

Click.

Couch available: Maybe
Age: 55
Grew up in: The Bronx
Ethnicity: New Yorker

Her answer to the last question made me stifle a laugh.

I read ahead to her Personal Description: "NOTE TO POTENTIAL COUCHSURFERS: DO NOT, I repeat DO NOT, message me without fully reading my couch information. It drives me absolutely NUTS when people try to use my space without even BOTHERING to read about my couch requirements..."

Uh oh.

I scrolled down to the "couch information" section:

Preferred Gender: Male.
Shared room: Yes.
Shared sleeping surface: Maybe.

"Couch surfers must be open to sharing a clothing-optional space..."

*

I clicked the back button quickly.

Profile #2:

I scrolled to find a picture of a baby-faced young man. He didn't look older than fifteen.

Click.

Couch available?: Maybe
Age: 20
Grew up in: Brooklyn

Education: I folow my on path.
Ethnicity: nun of ur fucking biznis!

Um, okay then. I skipped ahead to the couch information:

Preferred Gender: Any.
Maximum Number of Surfers: Any.
Shared room: Yes.
Shared sleeping surface: No.

"Hey everyone, so heer is the deel: I live with my parints, and theyre not too down with the hole CS thing so OBVIOUSABLY you MUST be willing to:

#1 – Stay in my room
#2 – Sleep on the floar
#3 – Pay me a small monitary compinsation of $30 a day to help me pay my tuishin fees…"

Click.

*

That was enough of that. I thought it was probably better if I joined an "NYC couch requests" group to see who would respond. So I found a group, typed up a general inquiry, and waited a full week for the requests to come to me.

They didn't.

I did, however, get a message from an old woman who was looking for a temporary tenant who would be willing to do her cooking and dry cleaning for a few days, and another from a young man who had actually received negative reviews on Couchsurfing.org, notably from females whom he had sincerely creeped out.

"Sam, what are your expectations for staying at my place?" he wrote.

I wasn't really sure if either of those counted as couch offers.

I was not yet ready to give up my dreams of going on a ~~low~~ no-budget road trip. If I took a morning Megabus, I could reach NYC at an ungodly hour, perhaps even before the city-that-never-sleeps woke up. If I could accomplish that, I could exhaust myself by touring around, take a really late-night bus out to Washington, and then sleep on that instead. A bus wouldn't be able to replace a bed on a nightly basis, but it would have to do in NYC.

I sent out requests on Couchsurfing.org, and I was easily able to find couch offers outside of New York. In fact, I didn't even really have to send out offers, because a lot of people reached out to me. The community was so giving and welcoming; it was truly a beautiful thing to be a part of, and made me want to give back in any way I could.

After making arrangements with a couple of people on the website, it was time to confess what I'd been plotting to my parents. Having an Indian background, I was used to my parents taking strict, hard-line stances. I worried that they would say no, especially when they found out that I had arranged to stay with young men.

When I first told them what I wanted to do, my parents were suspicious about the whole concept of couch surfing, and of solo female travel in general. But after I showed them the Couchsurfing.org website, I could see their minds start to change. I went over the website and the concept with them, and showed them the profiles of the people I planned to stay with. They already knew that I was an active member of LiveMocha.com, and that spending all that time in a virtual community like that had awakened a sense of wanderlust in me. Also, I think that with all of the anxiety I'd been internalizing, they could sense that this trip was something I needed. Miraculously, my parents gave me their blessing.

The person who took the news the harshest was actually Latoya, an old university friend of mine. Thanks to the internet, we still kept in touch. We were inseparable as students. She would sleep over at my dorm room at least once a week, where we'd have girls' nights in, complete with mani-pedis, nachos and/or popcorn, and scary movies. Then she graduated and went back to Grenada. Despite that she had studied abroad, she was terrified of international travel and worried for my safety. I promised to text her often.

I went online, selected a bus ticket from Toronto to NYC and clicked "buy." Judging by what I could see via the web about couch surfers and hostel prices, NYC was not a welcoming place for tourists, but I still couldn't wait to tour one of the most famous and beautiful cities in the world. And even if I hated it, it would only be a stop along the road on what had become a much bigger trip than I originally anticipated.

Just a couple of days before my trip, I noticed a seat sale on a plane ticket from Miami to Toronto for ninety-nine dollars. I snatched it up.

It was real. This was happening.

The night before I was set to go, I packed a tiny suitcase full of the cheapest, flimsiest of clothes. Sundresses. Shorts. Thin, baggy t-shirts. I needed to be able to fill the maximum amount of outfits into the smallest amount of space, not only so I would be able to lug it around, but also so that I had a decent amount of clothing combinations I could get through before I'd need a wash or have anyone notice that I was wearing the same things every day. Tank tops were golden because they could be worn with shorts or capris, or even under baggy shirts or dresses. Dresses were great because they took up a small amount of room, but could stand alone. If I was ever in a rush to get ready, I could throw a dress over my head and have a complete outfit. I decided to pack only boots and flip flops, no sneakers. Boots could be worn if it rained or if I wanted to make my capris look like pants, and flip flops could be worn everywhere else: in hostel showers, on the beach, and even around town. Sneakers were superfluous, and would take up precious room. I even waxed my legs before the trip so that I wouldn't have to pack a razor.

With this attitude in mind, I carefully packed only the most basic necessities—mostly clothes, along with a few key emergency items, such as toiletries (NO makeup), sunscreen, granola bars and puddings for emergency calories on long trips, homemade pepper spray (vinegar and cayenne pepper mixed together in a pocket-sized perfume bottle), chap stick, a ten-inch laptop, and two precious books: my journal, and *The Bhagavad Gita*.

My journal was empty. I had received it as a gift years before, but it was so beautiful that I had never dared to write in it. It was a navy blue, cloth journal, decorated with Eastern style batik flowers. It was time to fill it with the marks of experiences.

I made sure I had a camera with an empty memory card and a great classic rock playlist downloaded on my phone. Classic rock is the soundtrack of any good road trip.

I only brought two pieces of jewellery: a tulsi bead necklace and a heart-shaped locket I had bought for a dollar or so at Forever XXI. Inside the locket, I put a small picture of Radha and Krishna. Lord Krishna and His eternal consort Srimati Radharani were my protectors, friends, and well-wishers. While They always thought of me, I knew that my journey would be all the more auspicious if I made sure that I never forgot Them.

Bussing across the Border

The bus station was huge. I was still in my own city of Toronto, and I was already feeling lost. Accompanied by my ever-supportive parents, I got in line to ask the ticket salesman where I should stand to get on the bus to New York.

"Excuse me!" said a self-entitled grandparent, dragging his eight-year-old grandson along with him. He shot me a challenging look. "I'll only be a sec. I just need to ask a question. Thanks!" he said quickly, running in front of me and right up to the salesman before I could even open my mouth in protest.

After he left, I approached the booth.

"Hello, can you please tell me where to stand to get on the Megabus for New York City?"

The salesman looked bemused. "You weren't with that dude?"

"No! He just butted in front of me!"

The salesman laughed. "I thought he was witchu!"

"I know right? Who does that?"

"Ha ha...welcome to New York. That's a typical New Yorker right there. Ain't nobody gets a spot ahead o'dem. He's gonna be on the same bus as you, platform number four."

"Awesome, thanks."

I took my time heading over to the platform, taking a moment to wish my parents goodbye.

"Text, Skype, Facebook ...whatever you want, anytime!" said Dad. "We're always awake if you need to talk."

"It's the same time zone, Dad," I said with a laugh.

As we were about to part ways, mom reached into her purse to look for her car keys, and a stocky man with tattered clothing approached us, aggressively gesturing at my mom's purse and asking for change. Her purse was already out, and he'd caught us off guard during a heartfelt moment.

"Please—I just need money to get the bus back home to see my son!" he begged.

Mom handed him a couple of dollars, and he leered into her purse.

"More?"

"I'm sorry," said Mom sternly.

He left.

"*American*," said my dad under his breath.

"Are you sure?" I asked.

He nodded.

I gave my parents a quick hug and departed for the bus terminal.

Sure enough, there was that older gentleman from the lineup right in front of me. He was holding his grandson's backpack and baseball cap in one hand, his other wrapped around the young child. When the bus arrived, he rushed ahead of everyone, ensuring he and his son got the front seat of the bus. Why anyone would be picky about the view on a night bus was beyond me!

A shirtless, sweaty passenger who looked to be in his early twenties grabbed my suitcase and put it into the storage compartment for me, grunting.

"Hey thanks!" I said.

He did not respond.

I sat on the upper deck, near the back, intending to get some sleep. The top floor was already packed with a large group of at least thirty other tourists from who were speaking an East European language and swearing loudly in English, walking up and down the aisle half-clothed, and passing around a large plastic coke bottle that I was sure wasn't full of coke.

My phone buzzed. I thought that it was probably my parents, wanting to wish me one last goodbye on this side of the border.

I pulled it out of my pocket. I didn't recognize the number.

"Hi Samita...this is Arjun—Shyam's brother."

"Oh yeah, I know who you are. What's up?" I said coolly. Shyam and I had briefly dated—and it had ended badly. He was close with his brother, but I didn't think he told him what happened. It wasn't a very flattering story for either of us.

"Shyam told me you are looking for a job. Do you want to do something in my company? I just started a business! I realize I'd have to pay you, and I'm okay with that."

"Sorry Arjun, I can't. I'm about to leave for a vacation. See you later!" I said.

It felt good to turn down a job offer, albeit an unconventional one. I smiled to myself, and prepared to get some rest in my comfy sweatpants and t-shirt.

*

Once I put on my sleeping mask, the chattering of the other passengers quickly transformed into an incomprehensible droning sound. I'm not sure if it was the other passengers' voices, the whirring noise of the bus, or myself snoring, but I managed to fall into a shallow sleep for a couple of hours until I was rudely nudged awake by an overweight young man with curly brown hair.

"What?" I asked grumpily.

"Wake up!" he hissed. "They're calling us off the bus and unloading our luggage so that we can get searched and interrogated."

"Damn, I forgot about that. Stupid terrorists," I mumbled semi-coherently, as the large group on the double-decker began to change back into their clothes. I tried not to look.

The boy nodded emphatically at me as he bugged his blue eyes. "Before 9/11 I could go to and from your country and mine with no problem. *Even* on a bus. I've been on buses that were literally just waved through—no one had to get out! Now the whole bus is searched. *Ridiculous*! I had to buy a passport card; I couldn't afford a passport."

"A passport card?"

"It's like a passport for North Americans," he said, pulling his out. It was dated to '94.

"Cool," I said. "And wow, you're really young to be travelling alone."

"I'm from Buffalo. We always come to Canada on weekends or whatever just to have fun."

"Thanks," I said. I was too tired to be any more conversational.

*

"Everybody out!" announced the Megabus driver. "If your passport is not North American, this includes Europeans, Japanese, and Indians, you will be fingerprinted, so you may cut ahead of those with North American passports in the line. This will save us all time in the long run."

"This is my first time getting interrogated alone," I said to the friendly American boy as we waited at the back of the line, behind the European tourists.

"Meh, you'll be fine," he shrugged. "I've gone through this tons of times. Your people ask some ridiculous questions. I was once asked flat-out by a border official if I'd ever been to terrorist training camp–"

"—Terrorist training camp!?" I interjected loudly.

"*Shhh!*" he said, bugging his eyes once more. "Look, as long as you know who you are and where you're going, you'll be fine."

*

Our suitcases were opened and sifted through thoroughly. Underwear, tampons—you name it. Luckily, the guards didn't seem too interested in my faux-mace, and moved me along to the next section. My purse was searched, and another guard picked up a fruit salad I'd chopped into a plastic bag.

"We don't allow fruit across the border without a label...but since you cut it up like this and you're obviously going to eat it..." He shrugged and put it back into my bag, handing it over to me.

I then got out my passport and went over to the counter of an attractive police officer in his mid-thirties. He had a large brown eyes, bronzed skin, and a badge that said "Mendez."

"Did I call you here?" he asked.

"Oh...whoops!" I said, heading back into the line. I figured that maybe they had a special order they wanted us to go in, and it wasn't time for my questioning yet.

"No—it's fine!" he said, caught off guard. "Please come back."

I realized that he did in fact want to question me. He was just trying to pull a power trip on me first to make me feel uncomfortable, but once he noticed it had back-fired, he completely abandoned it.

"Where are you from?" he asked me.

"Tronno," I slurred. Border guards were sometimes suspicious of people who claimed to be from Toronto, but pronounced it too properly, as no real Torontonian would.

"Where are you going?"

"New York City."

He nodded. So far so good.

"What're you doin' there?"

"Sight-seeing."

"What sites are you seeing?"

"I actually want to tour around the entire eastern United States by bus," I said. "I'm not sure exactly what to see, but I'm starting with New York City."

"Alone?"

"Yes."

He gave me a funny look. "Why? Visiting friends or family, or...?"

"I'm going to stay with some friends I met online," I responded.

"Boyfriends?" he asked skeptically.

I laughed. "No, not boyfriends," I said. I had no intentions of marrying my way into U.S. citizenship, and I think that he could tell that I was being truthful, because he dropped it immediately.

"Okay. How did you meet these friends?"

"Couchsurfing.org. It's a networking website for travellers."

He thought I was weird, maybe a little crazy, but not a threat to national security.

"Do you have a return ticket?"

"You bet!" I said awkwardly.

"...May I *see* it?"

"Oh yeah!" I said, handing him the receipt for my flight back to Toronto. Thank God I'd bought it on a whim just a couple of days ago—the young man from the bus later told me that they wouldn't have let me in the country without it.

"Okay, everything looks good. Be safe," he said, with what looked like genuine concern. He handed me back my passport.

Phew! I was glad that was over.

I joined the line to re-board the bus right behind the young man I'd been chatting with. I checked my phone; fifteen minutes had passed. We had both begun, and finished a long interrogation process at the same time. It appeared that no one got special treatment at the American border, not even the Americans. At least I didn't have to get printed.

"Couch surfing!" he exclaimed. "You didn't tell me you were couch surfing! I heard you tell the guard over there. You must be pretty outgoing; I thought you seemed too shy for something like that."

"I am shy, but I like to push myself outside of my comfort zone."

"Why?"

I shrugged. "It's a good way to develop yourself."

The young boy and I started talking about self-development and religion. He was a Christian, and I told him that I was a Hare Krishna.

"I've heard of you guys!" he said.

I told him that he should give it a visit on a Sunday, when most locations offered free dinners. Then I showed him my copy of *The Bhagavad Gita* before we said our goodbyes. He had just reached home, and I had just left mine.

I sent a quick text to Latoya: "Crossed the border!"

"Watch out. Here's where it starts," she texted back cryptically.

*

A brunette who looked about my age and size boarded the bus, talking loudly on the phone. There were many empty seats, but she sat down right beside me, smiled, and continued her conversation with her mother regarding her car payments. (It isn't eavesdropping if the other party is yelling.)

Nice, I thought to myself. *Maybe it's time I bought a car, too.*

My mom often let me borrow hers, but it was getting older and had started causing trouble—especially if I had a job interview to get to.

Since I obviously wouldn't be able to sleep for as long as her conversation lasted, I decided to do some reading. I got out *The Bhagavad Gita*, but where were my glasses? I had just put them in my pocket...but now they weren't there.

Shit. I was going to be travelling blind as a bat in a foreign country.

I went through my purse. Not there. I stood up, but they weren't on my seat.

"Hang on mom, I'll call you later," said the girl beside me. She turned to me. "What did you lose?"

"My glasses."

"Oh shit! I'll help you find them."

I was surprised by her sudden kindness toward a stranger like me.

She used her phone screen as a flashlight while searching under our seats, and found the glasses on the ground.

"Are these yours? They're kind of scratched up."

"Yeah. It's okay. They were already like that."

"You can get pretty cheap ones if you order online."

"I can't do that now. I'm travelling."

"Oh...well there's always Wal-Mart," she said with a smile. "Where are you headed?"

"I'm touring around the eastern part of the country for a few weeks. How about you?"

"Oh wow. I'm just going to New York City to visit my sister, but I wish I had the guts to do something like that. What other places are you headed?"

"Washington."

"I love Washington! There's a lot to see there. Get ready to do a lot of walking."

"Also...Savannah."

"You're going to love the Spanish moss on all of the trees. Don't eat it, though."

"Um, okay. I won't."

She was pretty well travelled, at least within her own country. She chatted with me the entire night, so when I got off the bus at NYC at five in the morning, I had spoken more in a few hours than I had all week back in Canada, I had already met two new people, and I felt like I hadn't slept a wink.

A Navel Gazer in New York

I was now in one of the largest metropolitan centres in the world. Its look and feel was similar to that in my own home city of Toronto, but some things were definitely unique. For example, the modern, global city maintained some old-time traditions. Young men yelled on the street, hawking newspapers at those about to take the subway. Fire escapes were either built on the outside of apartments, facing the street, or minuscule ones were shared between two buildings that were only a foot apart. Grey-haired men in business suits still felt that their time was too precious to shine their own shoes. Besides, they could let someone else do it for them while they got caught up on *The Wall Street Journal*. Hot dog stands were placed meters away from small fruit and vegetable vendors: grocery shopping and a quick lunch on the go, all in one.

Where have I come? I wondered, as I stepped into Penn Station, looking for a public bathroom to brush my teeth and wash my face.

Everyone walked so fast that individual people seemed to be mere waves in a large ocean of a crowd. I felt like I could easily get swept away if I just let them carry me. I leaned against a wall at the station so I could have some temporary respite. I fished out my purse so I could find some American change for a Metropass, but the purse strap snapped. I tied it back together—a little tacky, but I didn't care. I could shop when I got back to Canada.

I approached the man behind the booth.

"Hello, can I put like...," I paused as I scrounged around for my change, "...Seven dollars on a Metropass?"

"I'll serve the next customer while I wait for you," he responded, as I stood their dumbfounded with my change and a wad of bills out. Apparently I hadn't spoken fast enough.

I waited my turn, and then I entered the subway station to find a group of policemen standing near the entrance. One of them requested to check my bag. The subway wasn't too busy, but it wasn't empty either. Some people were already on their way to work.

I decided that my first stop should be the Staten Island Ferry. It was a great way to get a killer view and a postcard-worthy picture of the Statue of Liberty for free.

When I exited the subway, I struggled awkwardly to lug my suitcase down the stairs as several people passed me by. After some time, one of them took pity.

"May I help you with your bags?"

"No, thank you," I said, with suspicion. This was clearly not a place where people were kind to strangers.

I made it down the stairs, where my bags were searched again by some other policemen. Then I boarded the ferry, which was soothingly empty and silent.

I took breathtaking pictures, leaning against the rails and feeling the wind in my face. I was alone now. Without anyone to talk to, I could truly appreciate the moment and what it meant to be travelling solo.

There she was, looking more majestic than any photograph could capture: Lady Liberty. I took as many shots as I could before the ferry passed her, and while I was convinced in my mind that each shot was better than the last, none of them came out quite right.

With the remainder of my quiet time quickly coming to an end, I decided to open my favourite book.

It is far better to discharge one's prescribed duties, even though they may be faulty, than another's duties. Destruction in the course of performing one's own duty is better than engaging in another's duties, for to follow another's path is dangerous.

—The Bhagavad Gita, 3.35

I underlined the final clause—"for to follow another's path is dangerous." Maybe it was okay that I didn't have everything figured out yet. Maybe it was for the best that I hadn't done what was expected of me.

My parents, PhDs in organic chemistry, were actually disappointed that I had chosen to study arts, but they still believed in me.

"You're going to write a bestseller," said Dad, when he caught me scribbling down an LGBT young adult novel at age nineteen.

"I don't know that this is New York Times material."

Dad was unphased. "Then write another one. Just keep going."

*

I got off the ferry, had my bags checked, walked around aimlessly for a couple of minutes, and got back on the ferry. I had no idea what to do or where to go, and didn't want to continue wandering aimlessly with my luggage. The real purpose of the Staten Island trip was in the ferry ride.

I took a bus to a library, where my luggage was checked once more. I thought it would be a good spot to get my bearings. I found a desk in a study area surrounded by college students, and opened my mini laptop. I could go to Central Park, the MET, Times Square, Grand Central Station...

I thought I'd start the day with another library, but not just any library—the New York Public Library. The pictures of the interior were gorgeous, with Michelangelo-style ceilings and grandiose architecture. It looked more like a museum than a library. I hopped on the bus and asked the bus driver where to get off, but she only rolled her eyes and grumbled something about tourists. Figuring I must be going the wrong way, I got off the bus and crossed the street, catching the one on the other side.

By the time I got to the Public Library and hulled my luggage up all those white stone steps, I felt lightheaded.

And then I read the sign at the top: No luggage.

I asked the guard at the front door if I could store my bags somewhere for a fee, but he responded with a curt, "Please leave, ma'am, or I'll get security."

I wasn't about to be deterred that easily. There were some street artists at the bottom of the steps, selling their artwork at tables they had set up. I approached an older lady, selling Asian style paintings.

"Hi, can I ask you a favour?" I asked.

"Sure, what is it?"

"Can I hide my stuff under your table while I tour the library? I'll be back really soon, I promise."

"Of course, dear," she said.

I ran up the steps with a burst of energy that came along with not having the burden of heavy luggage. The security guard gave me a quizzical look, then a shrug, and let me through.

I ran through all the rooms, up the stairs, and checked out all the paintings as quickly as I could before I left. I didn't want to inconvenience that nice painter, after all!

I had seen my second sight of the day! But it was only ten a.m., and I had a while to go. I started to feel faint; the thirty-degree heat, coupled with the heavy baggage was too much to bear without sustenance. I stopped at an ice cream truck by the bus stop, and had my first ice cream of the day. (All of the trucks in the city sold vanilla, chocolate, and strawberry ice cream for three dollars each. By the end of the day, I had tried all three.)

Now that I had seen a glimpse into the art world, I wanted to see more. I took the bus to the world-renown MET and hauled myself and my things up another set of steps quite similar to those at the Public Library. When I got to the top, I was greeted by the same sign: "no luggage."

I went back down and asked another street vendor if he wouldn't mind watching my things, but his response surprised me.

He clicked his tongue. "My friend got ticketed last week for doing that for someone. A hundred and ten dollars."

"Wow," I said. "Well, thanks anyway."

I went into a hotel lobby across the street.

"Hello, do you have a booking with us?" asked a tall, slim, well-dressed young woman who instantly made me feel extremely unkempt.

"No. I was wondering if you would be able to watch my luggage while I explore the museum across the street."

"I'm sorry. For security purposes we *can't* store luggage," she said. Her smile didn't fade as she spoke.

"Thanks anyway," I said again.

I pondered to myself. *There must be somewhere that I can just throw my stuff. Who would steal a small, locked suitcase, full of cheap clothes? No body.*

The MET just happened to be primely located right beside Central Park. I looked around for a large bush where I could hide the suitcase, but when I saw an empty bench, the temptation was too great. It was still morning, but I was exhausted, and it was nice to be somewhere a little less busy and a little more green. And because the whole point of my journey was to savor time spent alone, I indulged myself for hours on that bench. When I took off my backpack, I realized what an appealing pillow that backpack would make.

There is no possibility of one's becoming a yogī, O Arjuna, if one eats too much, or eats too little, sleeps too much or does not sleep enough.

—The Bhagavad Gita, 3.35

I awoke, feeling rested. But as I re-emerged onto the busy streets of New York, with all its lights, cabs, and billboards, I felt overwhelmed with exhaustion. Where else to go? It seemed as if I had walked around the whole island (and part of Staten Island), but when I checked how I was doing for time, it was only two p.m. I walked over to Grand Central Station, just to say I'd been there, and then grabbed another ice cream and took a bus to Times Square. The streets were getting even busier now that it was afternoon, and the bus was packed. I couldn't find a seat, so I stood near the exit.

The bus jerked to a stop suddenly.

"Ouch!" said a woman behind me. I had stumbled when the bus stopped, and stepped right on top of her open-toed shoes.

"I'm so sorry!" I said, patting her on the shoulder.

She said nothing, but instead gave me a look like she might swear or spit on me.

"Oh, come here," said another lady. She moved her bag and made space for me to sit. I was clearly a staggering danger to the other passengers when standing.

26

"Thank you," I said.

After a few moments, she spoke to me again. "Hey, do you even speak English?" she asked.

Speak it? Honey I majored in it!

"Yeah, I know English."

"Oh good," she said. "Most of you tourists don't even speak the language. And in a city like this, you can never tell who does and who doesn't."

I nodded awkwardly.

Walking around Times Square, I came upon Sephora. At that time in my life, I used to enjoy going to Sephora now and again to admire and test out the high-end, adorably packaged makeup, always wanting to treat myself but rarely indulging—unless of course it was lip gloss, my weakness. In fact, I'd bought a mineral lip gloss, untested on animals, at a Toronto location just a couple of days before my trip. I entered the store, complied with the manager who asked me to leave my luggage at the front, and thought I would take the opportunity to freshen up with a lip gloss sample. But then I saw a tiny, twenty-five-dollar bottle of baby blue Dior nail polish.

I snatched a sample bottle, and proceeded to carefully, shamelessly paint all ten of my fingernails in a thick double-coat before putting it back. After all, it's not like I would see any of these employees again. I waited a few minutes for my new manicure to dry before leaving the store. I still thought I looked a little bit messy and wind-swept.

"*Señora*! I like your style!" someone yelled to me on the street.

Really? What a weirdo.

I frowned and kept walking. A man in front of Ripley's was performing stunts with a voodoo doll and swallowing nails. Over by Abercrombie and Fitch, two buff young men sporting nothing but briefs modelled in front of the store. I was used to seeing half-naked women in advertising, but seeing the same situation with the gender roles reversed highlighted the outrageous dehumanization of the marketing tactic.

I bought my third and final ice cream of the day and went into a cafe, where I stayed for the remainder of my time in the city. I kept trying to coax myself out, but I had run out of energy. I'd seen Lady Liberty, the Public Library, the steps of the MET, Central Park, Times Square, and walked the famed streets of Park Avenue, Madison Avenue, Fifth...I even saw the Brooklyn Bridge (from a distance). There was more I wanted to do, but I hadn't accounted for how tiring it all would be, and how much of an issue it was to travel in a place like New York with luggage. I went in line to order behind a teenage girl in short shorts, who looked about fourteen. You could see the lower part of her butt cheeks sticking out of the shorts, and the three cute Latino boys working there chuckled and gestured at her when she wasn't looking. She took her coffee and walked out, blithely unaware that she'd just been the "butt" of a joke. I briefly considered confronting the boys, but ultimately decided against it.

I approached the counter.

The cashier cleared his throat and pulled himself together immediately. "*Hola*, how can I help you?" he asked.

"Can I have a strawberry smoothie?" I asked. I was parched.

"Sure. Is that all?"

I thought for a moment.

"And a salad."

There. That'll make up for all of the ice cream.

"Okay. That'll be—"

"—Wait! And a veggie sandwich. I think I'm going to be here for a while."

"Okay."

I claimed a booth for four entirely to myself and my luggage. I spent the next seven hours reading, eating, and surfing the net. I used the washroom several times to refill a water bottle, and also went up to the counter a couple of more times to buy a coffee and another snack. If I was going to take up so much table space in a place that busy and crowded, I thought I might as well try and give them good business.

Staying in the cafe, I had no need to show any more security personnel the contents of my luggage. By then, I had already become so used to opening and closing my bags that it started to seem almost routine to me, almost normal.

I kept to myself. The only interaction I had was with a friendly older couple. They came over to the table to introduce themselves and tell me about how they were travelling from Salem to celebrate their thirtieth wedding anniversary. Then they asked me where I was from and what I was doing, wished me well, and continued out the door with their drinks.

Believe it or not, even after spending all that time in that cafe, I still had three hours to kill until my bus to Washington was scheduled to arrive. I thought it would be a good idea to head over to the bus station anyway. It was cooler outside now, and I didn't really know where I was going so being early couldn't hurt. I packed up my things.

"I know your cafe gets pretty crowded. Thanks for letting me stay here so long," I said to the cashier before I left.

"No problem!" he said kindly.

In my baggy sweats, I was certain that no one laughed at me as I walked out. I found it funny that physical appearance can completely alter the way a person treats you, despite that on the inside, whether rich or poor, male or female, human or animal, we are all equal as souls.

A person is considered still further advanced when he regards honest well-wishers, affectionate benefactors, the neutral, mediators, the envious, friends and enemies, the pious and the sinners all with an equal mind.

—The Bhagavad Gita, 6.9

I made it to Port Authority fairly easily. The bus stopped just outside of the station, and there were two young men wearing bright orange coats, marching back and forth right in front of it. Their skin was so dark, it was just a shade above pitch black.

I sat on the curb.

"Miss, you CANNOT sit there!" said one of the young men, running up to me.

"Why not? My bus is supposed to stop here. Am I too early?" I made to get out my bus ticket, but he shook his hands with disinterest, looking ticked.

He proceeded to give me a long lecture about "the types of people who took the bus."

"So you see, we MUST board the elderly and those with disabilities first. Not you! You NEED to move!" he shouted in conclusion. He looked positively irate.

"Okay," I said. I moved over to the sidewalk a few metres away from the stop, and sat there instead. It was pretty dirty, so I sat on my suitcase.

Just after I arrived and marked my place, the group of shirtless Europeans from the morning bus arrived and sat behind me. This time, they were sharing a bottle of sprite.

"Hey! I remember you!" one of them said to me.

"Yes, that was me," I said with a smile.

I went back to my favourite book, and the hotheaded bust station attendant's co-worker made a beeline for me right away.

"WHOA! What is that?" he asked, in a thick African accent.

"This is *The Bhagavad Gita*. It's a conversation between God and a friend of His that we can apply to our everyday lives."

He whistled. "You Indians have so much culture."

Finally, someone realized I'm not a Latina.

"I'm from Nigeria. We don't have books and parades like this."

"Parades?"

"Yes. Every year, you people throw a big parade down the street."

I laughed. "You're probably talking about the *Ratha Yatra*. That's not just for Indians. Those parades take place all over the world, including in West Africa. You can join if you want, and you should also read this book. It's for everyone, too."

I handed him the book, and his eyes lit up.

"Who is this?"

"That's Krishna driving the chariot. And with him is his friend, Arjuna."

"You know, I really love God. I would love to read this book. Do you know where I could get a copy?" he asked, handing it back to me.

"You could read it online."

"Okay, thanks. I will read it," he said.

I sent another text to Latoya: "Leaving NYC."

"LEAVING? Hope you aren't going SOUTH!"

I rolled my eyes, and I boarded the bus on the bottom floor—away from the European tourists, but it was still far from quiet. Colleagues discussed business on what was obviously, for them, a redeye. Note to self: never again replace a genuine place to sleep with a night bus.

And when the ride finally ended, I would have to hop off and take the metro over to Maryland to meet my very first Couchsurfing.org host. Could I really just shake hands and get into a car with a total stranger?

I felt so nervous I could puke.

When Strangers Become Friends

When it was time for all of the passengers to exit the bus, I groggily dragged myself into the station. I had managed to drift off into a semi-unconscious state for a couple of hours, but even if the bus had been quiet, it would have been impossible to get anymore than that because it was air conditioned to such an extent that it was much too cold for slumber. I went into the station, brushed my teeth in the bathroom sink along with at least a dozen hazy European girls, and rested on a seat for an hour, waiting for the metro to open at five a.m. Meanwhile, the tourists hurried over to another platform to catch a train headed for North Carolina, where they were visiting a winery. I felt kind of sad for them because they had come all the way to the United States and were going to miss out on a hub like Washington. I also had a feeling that they would miss out on a lot more.

"Are you with them?" asked a security guard.

"No," I replied. "I'm alone."

There were signs around the station that advised against loitering, but I told her that I was just waiting for the metro to open, and I'd be on my way.

"Alright. Be safe!" she said.

Be safe.

I found the comment a little unnerving.

*

Using the Washington metro is not an intuitive experience. I tried to slide in the card I purchased, but it kept getting rejected and the revolving bar wouldn't turn for me.

"Do you know how to use this thing?" I asked a long-haired man on a bicycle, in line behind me.

He shrugged nonchalantly.

I squeezed myself around the bar, and he nodded at me approvingly.

Really? That's how to do it? Seems like a strange way to get into the metro, I thought.

When I got off at the station near the house of Keshav, my Couchsurfing.org host, I exited the way I had entered.

"Ma'am, that's not how you exit!" scoffed a metro worker.

She swiped my card for me, and handed me a map.

"Cool, thanks. Where's Union Station?" I asked her, out of curiosity. My host had forewarned me that that was a good starting station for tourists.

"Read the map, and you tell me," she said.

Still in Toronto mode, I pointed somewhere at the bottom of the map. But the station was not labelled "union."

She sighed. "No honey. It's here."

"Thank you."

I got out my pen and circled it immediately.

A tall, black, scantily clad woman pointed at me and started waving wildly, but said nothing. I looked over at her.

OH MY GOD!, she mouthed silently, *YOUR BAG!*

She gestured at her own purse and pointed to it, then gave me a thumbs-up.

YOUR HAIR!, she mouthed again, running her fingers through her own.

YOU!, she concluded, drawing a circle in the air, with a final thumbs-up.

"Um, thanks," I said aloud, fighting the temptation to thank her in mime. It was like that compulsive feeling you get when someone starts whispering for no reason, and when you stop to ask them "why are you whispering?"—you end up whispering, too.

I exited the station quickly and texted Keshav. He was already there, waiting for me in a black sedan. I hopped in without a second thought, relieved. My time in transit was over.

"Hello, nice to meet you Samita," he said, his eyes never leaving the road. He seemed to be driving in the direction of the university, and he looked just like his picture: olive skin, thin lips, and a well-built frame. He appeared to be who he said he was.

When we got to his campus residence, he gestured to a mattress on the living room floor. "Make yourself comfortable. I am going to go back to sleep, then in a couple of hours my roommate and I have class. Help yourself to whatever's in the fridge; you won't find any meat in there."

"Awesome, thank you so much," I said, touched by his hospitality. It takes a special kind of person to wake up in the early hours of the morning, just to pick up a stranger to invite into their own home.

Although I was far away from my family and loved ones, God was still close to us all.

The Supreme Truth exists outside and inside of all living beings, the moving and the nonmoving. Because He is subtle, He is beyond the power of the material senses to see or to know. Although far, far away, He is also near to all.

I sent a quick text to my parents, telling them all they would care to know:

"Safe in Washington with my first host, Keshav. He is not a creep."

Then I dropped my bags and hit the mattress. I was out the moment my cheek touched the pillow.

*

I woke up and checked my phone: it was two p.m. There was a note beside the mattress:

Samita,

I am leaving for school. Please help yourself with the food etc. You can find milk, cereal, etc. in the kitchen. Email/call if necessary. See you in the evening.

Keshav

After bathing away the weariness of the long journey and the dust of the New York streets, and having a short Skype session with my parents, I spent a few hours wandering around the University of Maryland campus. Because it was summer, there weren't a lot of students around, which was nice. It was a grand campus. It had rained the night before, and it was a foggy, humid day. Universities weren't built with the same grandeur in Canada, and we didn't have sororities or fraternities (not that that's necessarily a good or bad thing, just different). Exploring the picturesque buildings and beautiful campus fields and gardens made me feel kind of like Nancy Drew.

In front of one of the buildings, there was a statue of a turtle. A student told me that people liked to rub his nose for good luck, especially around exam time. I decided to join in on the ritual. What traveller couldn't use a bit of luck?

I noticed some of the people on campus taking a free student bus that drove around the University grounds as well as into the residences. I waited by a stop with a couple of students, and went in. The dreadlocked bus driver, who was obviously a student at the university, checked everyone's student ID cards when they entered, but neglected to ask me for mine.

"Wow, you're lucky!" said Keshav, when I entered the bus.

"Oh hi! Didn't expect to see you here!" I said.

"I could say the same for you. They always card me! You're a lucky girl."

"Well, I did rub the turtle's nose."

*

In the evening, I went to a nearby Mexican grocery store with Keshav and his roommate Sachin, who was taller, lankier, and darker skinned than he was.

"I want to do something nice for you both. What do you like to eat? I'll make it for you."

"Cake!" Sachin exclaimed. "A vegetarian cake—no eggs."

"No eggs, no problem," I said.

I was a great baker, and I loved to make vegetarian cakes for my family.

"Do you guys need me to buy anything for the cake?" I asked.

"No," said Keshav. "We have flour and sugar and all that stuff back home."

"Cool."

But when we got back to their house, I saw that the only thing that they had in their house was whole wheat flour.

"I can't make a cake with this. It will taste like bread," I said.

"Sorry—that's all we eat," said Keshav.

We couldn't have cake, so Keshav made a pizza for us instead. I watched as he prepared the pizza, including every topping in his fridge and every seasoning in his cabinets—the kitchen sink.

Before we ate the pizza, Keshav wanted to have an impromptu yoga session, and his roommate and I gladly obliged.

Perform your duty equipoised, O Arjuna, abandoning all attachment to success or failure. Such equanimity is called yoga.

—The Bhagavad Gita, 2.48

He led the yoga class with Sachin and me as his students, and pushed us into advanced poses, including arm binds and headstands. I thought I held my own pretty well, but Keshav kept insisting that I was doing all of the poses wrong.

"You should learn Hindi," he told me. "Then you could understand the poses better. You will always run into issues if you learn from Western teachers."

"Yes, India is the best country in the world!" interjected Sachin.

"I speak a little Bengali," I said.

"Ah, but Hindi is better. More people know it."

"Well, both Hindi and Bengali stem from Sanskrit. The poses are actually named in Sanskrit. A lot of Western teachers actually understand it."

"I understand it better," said Keshav.

"Oh, great!" I said. "Have you read *The Bhagavad Gita*? It was originally spoken in Sanskrit."

"No, but I know about it."

I found an audio version of the book in English on YouTube, and we played the wise words of God in the background as we ate the pizza. My stomach started to grumble; the pizza didn't sit well with me.

"You're probably just not that used to Indian style pizza," said Keshav nonchalantly.

It was definitely true that my tummy wasn't used to all that spice. I promised I would help him out in the kitchen from then on.

Before bed, Keshav helped me to pre-register to tour the Capitol Building, and warned me that security would be tight. He told me to pack light if I didn't want my things thrown in the trash.

Walking Through Washington

The next morning, I was up early. I donned an Obama t-shirt that I had bought in Canada and planned to wear specifically on this trip. Besides, I was in a blue state, and I might not have another chance to wear it once I headed further south.

I took the campus bus to an intersection where I could get a city bus to a metro station. A petite woman jumped off the bus behind me and walked up to me.

"Do you know how to get to the metro?"

"I do. That's where I'm headed. Follow me."

I told her that I was couch surfing, and she told me that it was something she had tried in the past. Then she told me about WWOOFing, an opportunity that allowed people to stay on organic farms around the world and learn about sustainable living.

I got off at Union Station and wished the girl good luck. I hadn't come up with a plan for what to do once I got there, so I wandered aimlessly for a bit, ending up in Chinatown.

"Obama!" yelled a young man on the street, pointing to my shirt.

"Obama!" I shouted back.

"Here's hoping for another four years," he said, before walking away.

I wandered into a crime museum. Ted Bundy's car was displayed right in the front. I shuddered with the thought of all of the women who may have died in that car.

At the front desk, I saw that there was a fee to enter the museum, so I didn't go in. I did, however, grab a complimentary map of the vicinity.

Now that I knew where I was, I could figure out where to go. I sat down on the steps of a small art gallery, and circled all the places of interest: Capitol Hill, the Library of Congress, the Smithsonian, National Archives, the National Gallery of Art, the Washington Monument, and the White House—basically, I needed to see the entire three-kilometre stretch of the National Mall. Because Capitol Hill required pre-registration, I decided to do it first. That meant I would have to retrace my steps a bit, as people in judge's cloaks strutted past me. I was having the vacation of a lifetime, but this was where people lived and worked—right beside the White House, the residence of President Obama at the time.

On the grassy field of what is known as the National Mall, I waited in line to enter the building. A guard searched our bags, and told us that if we had anything to eat, we'd better eat it now or throw it in the dumpster that was just behind her. Although I wasn't hungry, I wolfed down my granola bar and emptied my water bottle onto the manicured green grass. I felt really bad for the person in front of me; he had brought a professional camera with lenses and lens cleaners. He had to dump all of his cleaners.

The capitol building had enormous mural-sized paintings of key political figures, as well as large white statues of representatives from every state. There was a painting of Pocahontas getting baptized, and many statues of Indian chiefs as well as former presidents.

"Who do you think that this is?" asked the tour guide, pointing to a statue of Lincoln.

"Lenin!" joked a smart-alecky boy. He couldn't have been more than ten.

41

"No, it's Lincoln. Why would you say it's Lennon?" asked the guide.

"Oh, I know who it is. I just thought it would be funny to have a statue of the most anti-democratic figure in a place like this."

"Oh *Lenin*!" she said. "I sincerely thought—and hoped—you meant John Lennon. If any of the states wanted to have a statue of Lennon as their representative, it would be more than fine with me." She smiled.

In the Library of Congress, I had my bag searched again and was asked to lose my gum before entering. That's where I saw it: the original Declaration of Independence. I also saw several first editions of classic American books.

"Have you read that one?" asked a middle-aged man who was beside me.

"No, but I've heard of it."

"It's amazing."

"Thanks. I'll look into it."

"Have you read *that* one?"

This went on for a little bit, until he eventually gave up after realizing that I hadn't read most of the American classics. I had considered myself fairly well read, but now I saw that I had a lot more work to do. I made a note to self to read more books when I returned home. (Of course, the best book of all was in my hand bag the entire time.)

My phone buzzed.

"Where r u now?" Latoya texted.

"Washington. Staying with a host."

"A host?"

"Met online."

"R U TRYING TO GIVE ME A HEART ATTACK!?!"

"Love u. Talk later."

After leaving the Library of Congress, I went to a water fountain to refill my empty bottle.

O son of Kuntī, I am the taste of water.

—The Bhagavad Gita, 7.8

The delicious taste of water quenched my thirst completely. Nothing was more satisfying than the taste of God!

There were some ice cream stands selling fudgsicles where I could also have gone if I wanted to cool down, but after my overindulgence in New York, I thought it wiser to restrain myself. A couple of zits, undoubtedly from the chocolate ice cream, had already crept their way through the skin on my forehead, and I was covering them with my hair. I've always been extremely reactive to chocolate, so I've learned over the years to pretty much live without it. The only part of my body that chocolate agrees with is my tongue.

Beside the fountain, a couple of boys were skateboarding on the sidewalk.

"Hey!" I called to them.

"Yeah?"

"Do you know which way to the Washington Monument?"

"Nah!" they yelled back, and made off.

I would have to stop being lazy. I dug into my purse and pulled out the map, and saw the Washington Monument located a few blocks westward. I hopped on a bus, and scrambled for change. All I had were bills.

"I can help you out!" said a short woman with tanned skin. She had wide, amber-brown eyes, full red lips, and a large nose. If her features were only slightly smaller they would look captivating, but they were each so big that she looked a bit strange.

She helped me break my bills, and we made a bit of small talk. She told me that she was from Serbia.

"I knew you weren't from here, either. I feel you—I had the same problem when I was new. But now, I always have change for the bus."

"Thank you so much!" I said.

When I first laid eyes on the Washington Monument, I was taken aback by its colossal size. There was no way those skater boys could have missed it. Maybe they just didn't know what it was called.

Or maybe a sight that seemed so wondrous to me was just so mundane to them, just another object to pass on their skating route, an everyday part of their environment.

Know that all opulent, beautiful and glorious creations spring from but a spark of My splendor.

—The Bhagavad Gita, 10.41

I vowed to myself to never lose the sense of admiration I had for any of Krishna's creations. Wherever my travels brought me in the future, I would always allow myself to stop and take in the beauty of the world around me.

44

I spent the majority of the rest of the week either on the metro (which I had by then become quite adept at using) or strolling through the National Mall. Those three kilometres may as well have been twenty, because Constitution Avenue and Independence Avenue were lined with national landmarks. All of these free, world class museums were full of stories from the past to tell. Every day, I would return to Keshav's with my feet aching. He assured me that he'd hosted enough travellers to know that it was a common symptom among Washington's tourists.

I managed to see the Abraham Lincoln and Martin Luther King Jr. memorials, but I never made it to see the Jefferson memorial, which required a long walk across a bridge. At least I was able to take a great shot of it, overlooking the Tidal Basin.

Outside the National Museum of the American Indian, gardens were laden with sculptures of teepees, and street performers played the drums on upside down buckets. Inside the museum, the most interesting exhibit of all was the live performance that I was lucky enough to catch firsthand. The first group performed what they called a "Bear Dance," explaining that in ancient times, humans were able to communicate with animals. The fact that we no longer can speaks to our own shortcomings, not theirs.

"In this dance, the women pick the partners," said the announcer, as female dancers initiated and lead the dance with male performers. Then, the male performers cleared out, and the women handpicked men from the audience to dance with them.

The next performance was by a Polynesian dance group. They wore wraps that were similar to Indian *dhotis*, and wore crowns of flowers in their hair. It was nice to see the interconnectedness of cultures around the world.

The dancers invited anyone from the audience who wanted to join, and I hopped on stage! They walked us through the steps.

When I left the stage after the performance, a woman approached me. She had wise, kind eyes, lined with the crow's feet of someone who had lived a full and happy life.

"Great dancing! Are you Indian?" she asked me.

"Well, actually I'm Canadian, but you could say that."

"Is your necklace Indian too? What tribe is that from?"

I realized that she was referring to my tulsi necklace. I told her that I was not Native; the necklace was made from the wood of a sacred tree in India, the favourite tree of Lord Krishna.

"It's so beautiful!" she said. "Is it expensive?"

"Not at all."

In the art museums, I saw dozens of portraits by George Catlin, the first white person to draw Natives in their native territory. His mother had even been captured by a tribe, and encouraged his interest in Native culture. I also saw an original painting of Queen Elizabeth I, and a beautiful fountain with a statue of a girl wringing her hair. The water from the bottom of her hair dripped back down into the fountain.

In the African Art Museum, I admired some sculptures from Cameroon. Art galleries always evoked my wanderlust, even when travelling. I imagined myself on the beach of a coastal African country, ~~speaking French~~ putting some rusty high school courses to use...

Comment allez-vous?

Je viens de Canada.

Je suis perdu.

Où est la salle de bain?

46

That was when I came across the most haunting thing I saw on my entire journey. I could feel the vibrations emanating from the other side of the room. I moved toward it, and read the description below the carved face. It was a voodoo mask from the late nineteenth to early twentieth century Bamum people in Cameroon. I thought of all the powerful spells that must have been cast using this mask in its heyday, their effects still resonating in this eerie carving...

*

"Awful! Despicable!" said an elderly white man standing beside me in the Smithsonian National Museum of American History. He gestured at a pair of miniature handcuffs made to shackle enslaved infants. He was shaking his head and practically spitting with disgust.

"Well, at least now America acknowledges the—"

"—Amen!" he interjected, nodding vehemently.

To my own surprise, I did not share his sense of ire. The year before this trip, I had explored West Africa with some other students, as part of a field trip organized by my university. We visited Elmira, a Ghanaian "slave castle," and the aura of the horrific place was so disturbing that I was ruined for the rest of the day. I still remember the smell in the air when we entered the women's chambers, which was really just a prison. Worst of all was the presence of a church in the center of the castle grounds. It was truly a tragic sight to behold.

But a year later, as I perused the Smithsonian in Washington, DC, I saw the acknowledgement of Jefferson's hypocrisy at an exhibit called "Paradox of Liberty." I noticed the exhibition's thoughtful rhetoric: Jefferson's Monticello residents were "enslaved people"—not slaves.

"The Promise of Equality and Democracy," read a placard at one of the exhibits. "Though the Declaration of Independence stated that 'all men are created equal,' race, religion, ethnicity, class, and gender limited the rights of many Americans to participate in the Constitution's promise of democratic government. African Americans and women struggled throughout the nineteenth century for rights that only white male property holders had been granted in the eighteenth century."

A mask of an African caricature was displayed as a target formerly used at the Coney Island fair until far too recently. The information box also revealed that the mask replaced the use of a real black person's face.

I saw this acknowledgment of the struggles of women and black people as a step forward. That national museums would integrate the darker parts of history into their exhibits in a genuine way, and not with condescension, was surely a positive thing.

The National Museum of American History also featured the original Star-Spangled Banner. There was a lineup to see it, glass-encased, in low lighting. It needed the protection, as squares from the corner of the flag had already been cut out, probably passed down as heirlooms or mistakenly thrown in the trash by those who had been gifted the flag fragments.

In the Smithsonian National Museum of Natural History, I saw the Hope Diamond, encased in glass walls, set on a necklace, and spinning on a pedestal. People crowded around to capture its amazing sparkle in a photograph. The diamond is estimated to be worth up to three hundred million dollars.

Originally from India, the diamond has exchanged hands many times in its history, each time getting a little bit smaller. Most of the people who have acquired it have wound up dead, usually murdered.

The Smithsonian traced the diamond's history by about three hundred years, but legend has it that the stone may have been the Syamantaka Jewel, a jewel that Lord Krishna helped to recover for King Satrajit about 5,000 years ago. Others say that the famed Syamantaka is actually a ruby.

*

"Do you think that the Hope Diamond will ever be returned to India?" I asked Keshav and Sachin over a dinner of rice and dal during my final night in their dormitory. As a side dish, I had helped them to prepare *boras*, a recipe that my father taught me, originating from the villages of Bengal. It was basically sliced and breaded pan-fried vegetables. I told them that similar methods could be used for homemade veggie burgers.

Keshav nodded. "Some day, I think India's jewels will all be returned. But at least for now, it's in the Smithsonian.

"Where it can't curse anyone?" interjected Sachin, jokingly.

"That, and it's better than having it around the neck of a socialite or anything like that."

I loved the way that couch surfing granted you an instant friendship. Within the first few hours of meeting Keshav and Sachin, I felt like I had been friends with them for years. In fact, I was already speaking more freely with them than with a few of my friends from home.

I was ready to embark on the next part of my journey, but I no longer felt alone. Although I had savored my solitude, there was a big difference between enjoying time to myself and feeling lonely. I had no reason to feel lonely because Lord Krishna, my friend and ever well-wisher, was with me the entire time.

I am the father of this universe, the mother, the support and the grandsire. [...] I am the goal, the sustainer, the master, the witness, the abode, the refuge and the most dear friend.

—The Bhagavad Gita, 9.17, 9.18

Deep Conversations on the Way to the Deep South

I bought a paper cup of vanilla ice cream from Washington's Union Station before making my way to the Greyhound bus station, located a couple of blocks away. When I stepped outside, I realized how chilly it was; it was actually drizzling a little bit. It was so windy that I took shelter in a doorway while I got my things together—putting some unnecessary items in my suitcase and making sure that my bus ticket was easily accessible. I mildly regretted treating myself to such a large ice cream cup during this foul weather.

"Can I have your soup!" a large, intimidating homeless man shouted at me.

It was more of a demand than a question, and he was already heading toward me, leering hungrily at the cup of ice cream in my hand.

Caught off guard in a vulnerable position with my bags hanging open, I practically threw the ice cream at him. He was already reaching for it.

"You can have it!" I said quickly, before I had even fully registered what happened.

He ran off, and I was just relieved that he hadn't asked for anything more. At least I no longer had to worry about how I was going to finish all that ice cream. And, I had offered the food to Lord Krishna before I started eating it, so the ice cream that he ate was blessed.

It was only as I began to walk toward the station, reflecting on the incident and calming my nerves, that I realized that he lunged at the ice cream hoping for soup! It was a bit cold, especially for July, and he would probably be disappointed when he found out that the soup was actually ice cream.

More homeless men stood in front of the doors to the bus station, blocking the entrance.

"Excuse me," I said.

They reluctantly moved away, and I hauled myself through the door, along with my semi-broken handbag, a backpack, and a suitcase. I sat down, placed my bags beside me, and got out my journal so that I could write down all of the things I was looking forward to doing in Georgia. The first thing I wanted to do was take a nice, long shower. I had arranged to pamper myself during the first night, where I rented a room in a fancy bed and breakfast. I told the person who would be hosting me for the next couple of days afterwards to pick me up at the hotel in the morning. It would be good to have some time to surcharge before meeting him. I was by nature an introvert, and I found it exhausting to be social, even when I enjoyed the company.

There was an office in the station with glass walls, where an attendant sat behind a desk. The sign in front of the door read "SECURITY/SEGURIDAD," but somehow, I still didn't feel too secure. Greyhound stations were invariably creepy. I felt a buzz.

Latoya texted: "Try not to get sold into modern slavery. I know a story..."

Thanks, I thought to myself, in no mood to text back.

*

All was well from the moment I entered the bus.

"Here's the deal," announced the bus driver. "No drinking alcoholic beverages, no smoking in the bus bathrooms, and no illicit substances of any kind—even if you're willing to share with me. No Skyping loudly or talking loudly on your cell phone. If the person on the other line requires you to scream, time to suck it up and buy a more expensive phone. Oh, and most importantly, absolutely *NO* talking to me when I'm driving, or I'll ignore you as if you were my own ex-wife."

The passengers chuckled, and I began to relax as I prepared for slumber.

Still, I wondered to myself, *No smoking, no drugs? Did these things really require a formal statement?*

Apparently I had no idea what I was in for on this bus trip destined for the faraway land of Georgia.

For example, back where I came from, a woman on the bus who is holding a book in her hand, or who has her eyes covered with a sleeping eye patch is sending a clear warning to other passengers to leave her alone. Or else.

In America, it is seen as a great opportunity for discussion.

"Hey there ma'am. Whatcha readin'?" an elderly gentleman with a Southern drawl may ask.

The women are no better: "You look mighty tired. Where'd you come from?" a Southern belle may inquire.

An eye patch is hardly a drawback. If anything, it's an invitation.

*

I awoke from my jostling slumber when I received a sharp poke in the arm.

I reluctantly took off my eye patch and groaned at the woman in front of me.

"This seat taken, hun?"

I moved my purse so she could have a seat, then promptly readjusted my eye patch, wishfully, but all too soon.

"So where you from?" the woman started. "Ya Indian?"

"*Uhhhhhh,*" I affirmed/groaned.

"Mmmmhmmmm," she said, extending the "*hmmm*" with an endearing emphasis. "I knew it. Cherokee?"

I thought for a moment. But alas, there was no way of avoiding this conversation. I sat up and lifted my eye patch.

"The other kind of Indian."

"Oh!" she said excitedly. "India! The weather down there suits a belle like me just fine! Do y'all really wear those dots on your foreheads? And those wrap dresses?"

"For special occasions," I responded curtly.

"I bet they look mighty pretty on you," she replied, mollifying me. *Maybe a late-night conversation with a nosy passenger isn't so bad after all?*

"So what brings you to the West?" she asked.

"Actually, it's what's brought me to the South," I said. "I'm from Canada."

"Oh," said the woman bemusedly. "But you said you were Indian?"

She pronounced the word as if it were three syllables long: *In-di-an.*

"My mother is part Indian," I clarified. "I was born in Canada."

"Oh my," she said. "A Northerner? Bless your heart."

She patted me on the shoulder, visibly less interested.

Did she really just bless-your-heart me for being Canadian? I laughed to myself. I should have put my eye patch on right then. But what can I say? I kind of liked the attention.

I shrugged. "Well, I've been to India."

The woman perked up again. "Really? What's it like there? I always done wanted to go, what with my sister getting outsourced down there. But then we had a falling out two years ago, and now I'm always scared I'd run into her. She's up in *Moom-bai*. Where were you?"

"Calcutta."

"Is that near Moom-bai?"

I sighed. At any other time I would have found this woman's unique combination of curiosity and cluelessness charming, but my exhaustion was starting to catch up with me. I needed to cut this conversation short.

"Look," I said, "if you really want to go to India you should go. It's an amazing country with a billion people. You won't be found by anyone that you don't want to find you. I hope you go someday, and I'm sorry, but now I really should be getting back to—"

"—A *billion*?!"

"*Shhhh!*" wheezed a faceless voice from behind her.

"Oh dear, I'm just a small-town woman. I don't know if I could go to a place with a billion people..." she trailed off.

We heard a noise from the front. An old man cleared his throat.

"Everybody praise *Jeeee-sus*!" he belted. He had a deep throaty voice that was actually quite pleasant to the ears.

That still didn't change the fact that it was ten in the evening. On a Greyhound bus.

"Jeeee-sus! I said Jeeeeeeee-sus! Everybody praise the Loooooord!" He crooned.

When no one reacted, he decided to take it a step further, and began to clap his hands.

"Sir?" said the bus driver, with an accent as northern as mine. "Please refrain from singing. People are trying to sleep."

"You don't like that song?" responded the elderly gentleman coolly. "I'll sing another."

"Please sir, do not," replied the bus driver.

The old man grumbled obscenities, eventually falling silent.

I thought that by now, I knew the drill: wait in line indefinitely, listen to the bus driver test out his comedy routine, prepare to wash your hands with sanitizer in lieu of soap and water, and brace yourself for random conversations with various colourful characters—but even I, a seasoned bus traveller—could not have anticipated encountering someone like him. Angered that his singing wasn't appreciated, he shuffled up and down the bus aisle, swearing and knocking people as he passed them.

"Ow—watch yourself!" a passenger shouted. Most of us just ducked.

"Now I've heard everything," I whispered to the woman beside me.

"My sister can be a real pain in the ass," she responded, unaffected by the man's outburst.

"What?"

"My sister. The one down in *In-di-a.* I invited her over to my house a couple of years ago, and she behaved *real* bad."

It was a lesson that would serve me well once I arrived in the Deep South: when nosy people get too interested in you, get them talking about themselves.

She proceeded to tell me intimate details about her relationship with her sister, things that were said, and things that were left unsaid between them. I felt myself nodding off...I checked my phone, and it was now almost eleven at night.

I tried once more to cut her off. "Ma'am," I began—I was starting to get accustomed to American etiquette—"I'm sorry, but—"

"Oh my!" she said, looking at my cell phone. "Would you look at the time? Have we really been talking until eleven?"

Well, you have, I thought to myself.

By the time I had put my phone back in my pocket, the woman was snoring. I decided to get on it myself, but we soon had to deboard for our first pit stop in North Carolina, my seatmate's final destination. She gave me her email and asked me to write to her and send pictures of my trip.

"Be safe," she said.

*

The bus stop had a seedy vibe, and I actually missed my temporary friend. A couple of homeless people had approached me rather aggressively at the Washington terminal, and I had trouble saying no. I looked around for a friendly face. I saw a short, stocky black man in an army uniform, and I took the seat beside him.

"Hi, I'm Samita," I said.

"Nice to meet you, sweetie. I'm Joe," he said, with just a soft hint of an accent. A smile broke across his tired face.

"Are you in the army?" I asked him.

"Yes ma'am!"

Awesome. No one will mess with me now!

A man approached us. "Do you know how I can get to Texas?" he asked my new friend, without a trace of a Spanish accent.

Joe responded in swift, fluent Spanish. I couldn't catch a word.

"Oh, you're Latino!" said the man, before continuing the remainder of their discussion in their native tongue.

After he left, Joe turned to me once more. "Are you Spanish, too? We can speak Spanish if you like."

"No, I'm not," I confessed. "You could speak to me in Spanish, but if you want me to reply, it's better if we just speak English."

He smiled again. "Of course."

"Excuse me, the both of you," said a man in old, dirty clothing that smelled of alcohol. His skin was the texture of leather. "I was wondering if you would be able to spare some change to help me get home to my family."

I already started reaching for my wallet, when the man continued.

"I'm a good person, I really am. I'm just trying to turn my life around..."

He trailed off, and Joe immediately gave him a dollar. I followed suit.

"God bless you both! Would I be able to trouble you for just one more dollar? It's very important that I get home to my family. They're expecting me, and I'm a changed man now..."

"Of course!" said Joe, passing him another George Washington.

The man hobbled off, asking some other passengers. They shook their heads without even looking him in the face. I wondered how he was so easily able to get me to empty my pockets. I thought that no one would approach me if I was with Army Joe, but he'd instead managed to get both of us!

"You've got to give people like that a chance," Joe said to me, in earnest.

I nodded seriously, but on the inside I was laughing at myself.

"Anytime I get the chance to help the less fortunate, I take it. That's why I joined the army," he told me.

"Good for you," I responded.

We stopped once more at a gas station in the early morning. I didn't even know which state we were in. It wasn't windy or rainy—it was hot again, and the landscape looked different. There were palm trees.

"Get out if you like, but don't be more than five minutes," said the driver, before he stepped out himself.

I ran into the gas station and used the restroom. It felt great to be able to wash my hands and face with soap! It was a luxury that most long-distance buses went without. I didn't brush my teeth this time. Instead, I bought a veggie sandwich, ran back to the bus, and wolfed it down. I wasn't sure where to get food in Savannah, so I thought it would be better to arrive with a full stomach.

*

Joe gave me a nudge. "There you are sweetie: Savannah, Georgia," he said, with his kind, gentle smile.

I rubbed my eyes. For the first time on my journey, I had actually slept on a bus. I wasn't just dozing, or pretending to sleep to avoid conversation—I was out cold. Being jolted awake from a deep sleep is difficult, but I was so excited to arrive that it was worth it.

I felt bad for Joe. He still had a painfully long journey ahead to an obscure small town, and this was following a plane ride. I admired how he held himself together like such a gentleman, even after such arduous travel. He was the epitome of stoicism.

Slow-Paced Savannah

At ten a.m. on a Sunday morning, Savannah was a ghost town. I had more than a few hours to kill before my check-in at three in the afternoon, but there wasn't much to do. I lugged my suitcase past the abandoned buildings and empty fields on the outskirts of the town, and into Savannah proper. Cars lined the streets outside of churches. I could hear the church bells ringing.

A quaint looking city bus pulled up beside me. Save for the driver, the bus was entirely empty.

"Are you okay?" he asked.

"Yes, thank you."

"Where you headed?"

"Just going to check in at a hotel."

"All the hotels are quite a ways. You sure you don' need no help?"

"Oh no, that's fine. I'm a tough girl."

He laughed. "Okay then."

*

The hotel was old and majestic. It used to be a mansion owned by a rich Southern family, but almost two hundred years after it was built, it had been converted into a business run by a couple. I was standing on the sidewalk, taking a five-second rest before I got ready to haul myself and my bags up the stairs, when one of the owners, a zaftig forty-something brunette, opened the door.

"Hello!" she said cheerily.

"Hi, I booked a room for the evening."

"Samita?"

"Yes!"

"I remember. Let me take your bags," she said, running down the steps and grabbing my bags before I could even hand them to her.

I had spoken to her on the phone when I booked the room from Canada, and I recognized her voice. That was probably my first time speaking to anyone with a charming Southern drawl. Now, it seemed common.

"Oh, you don't need to take the bags..."

"I insist!"

"Alright then!" I said, relieved. I was getting a bit tired, walking around with all of my things in the scorching Southern heat.

"I know that check-in isn't until three, but I didn't know where else to go. I was on a bus for about fifteen hours."

"You walked here from the bus station?"

"Well, yeah..."

"Oh heavens! Let me see...The guests who booked your room last night ain't left yet, but I'll tell one of the maids to get started as soon as soon as they check out. Do you have a number? I'll call you when it's done, and for now you can leave your bags with us behind our front desk while you walk around, get acquainted with the town, and wait for us."

She handed me a map.

"Thank you so much!"

"It's no problem. You must also be hungry. Why don't you go on down to the courtyard? We still have food from our breakfast buffet outside."

"Anything vegetarian?"

"Oh my...We ain't got too many of y'all down here, but I imagine you could have some cereal."

"That's perfect. I'm starving."

She nodded empathetically. "Go ahead and help yourself to breakfast. It's technically only for check-ins, but we'll just keep this between you and me."

I smiled. *Southern hospitality.*

The courtyard featured stone pathways and a fountain with a koi pond. Although the owner had worried me, the breakfast buffet had sundry vegetarian options, including toast, muffins, cereal, grits, yogurt, milk, juice, and tea. I had a glass of orange juice, and for the first time in my life, tried some grits. It was nice to be in the shaded courtyard, but soon the maids would come to clean up, and I would have to venture back out into the heat.

I was already feeling a bit faint at this point, and I didn't want to take any risks. I took a couple of pieces of toast, made myself a peanut butter and jelly sandwich, wrapped it up in some napkins and placed it choicely into my handbag. Before setting off, I clandestinely watered a courtyard tree with the remainder of water in my bottle, and filled it up with OJ from the buffet.

In a town where they ain't got many vegetarians...that should hold me.

*

I walked from the hotel to one of Savannah's major tourist attractions: Forsyth Park. On the way, I made a mental map of the city and where things were: a convenience store on one corner, a church on the other...

"Hey *gaw-juss!*" said an old man.

Without stopping, I laughed out loud and shook my head, and he giggled a little bit too as I passed him by. He walked slowly, as did everyone else—at least, the few people that I came across. Even the cars seemed to drive slower in the South, scarcely exceeding thirty kilometers per hour.

I took shelter under one of Forsyth's ancient live oak trees, with spooky Spanish moss draped over its copious branches.

The Supreme Personality of Godhead said: It is said that there is an imperishable banyan tree that has its roots upward and its branches down and whose leaves are the Vedic hymns. One who knows this tree is the knower of the Vedas.

The real form of this tree cannot be perceived in this world. No one can understand where it ends, where it begins, or where its foundation is. But with determination one must cut down this strongly rooted tree with the weapon of detachment. Thereafter, one must seek that place from which, having gone, one never returns...

—The Bhagavad Gita, 15.1, 3–4

I had just had breakfast, but I was already ready for my PBJ lunch. A squirrel scurried over to me, and I broke off a small piece of bread to share with him.

I wondered about the place from which we never return. I already felt like I was in such a foreign place, but I was soon to return. Going somewhere from which I would never return sounded ominous, but I reminded myself that things are often not what they seem. I tried to imagine a place so wonderful, that after going there, I'd never want to return to the material world, in all its misery, beauty, and glory. A place where water was nectar and the soil was composed of touchstones. Where every gait was a dance and every word was a song.

I was enjoying my time basking under a tree in a quaint and quiet town. I could get used to the pace. It was nice to take some time to relax, let myself melt in the hot sun, walk slowly, speak slowly...

Ouch!

A large, inch-long fly took a chunk out of my arm. I screamed out loud and smacked it, but it flew away before I could do it any fatal damage. I never tried to kill any uninvited house bugs I found sauntering curiously around my den, but when something tried to suck my blood or eat my flesh, it was another story.

"Oh my God, hun!" cried a fashionable young man, pedalling a rickshaw. He stopped and turned to me, flipping his stylish blonde hair, greased and side-parted. I guessed he was a student at SCAD, the Savannah College of Art and Design.

"What was that? A cicada or something?"

"No hun, I don't know what they're called...but they've come for me too. I feel you, boo!"

He pedalled away. I found it unusual that a town with so few cars on the road would have a rickshaw business going.

My phone rang.

"Hello, Samita?"

"Yes, this is she. Is my room ready?"

"You bet it is, honey. Come on over whenever you're ready."

I got up immediately. Maybe trees in the material world were overrated.

"Do you want your picture taken by the Forsyth fountain?" a man asked me.

"No thank you."

"Can't imagine why a girl like you don't want her picture taken."

"Goodbye," I said, and continued on my way.

I made it a point not to offer my camera to anyone who approached me asking for a photograph. If I ever wanted my picture taken, I was the one who asked.

When I got back to the hotel lobby, the other owner was there to sign me in. He was tall and lanky, with curly, dark brown hair. As he walked me up the stairs and to my room, he gave me the third degree.

"Oh, hello there. Let me show you to your room. Is this your first time in Savannah? How do you like it?"

"So far, I love it. It's very beautiful and peaceful."

"Let me see here...*Samita Sarkar*...Are you Spanish?"

"No."

"Indian? You're Indian! I just love Asha Bosul. She's the best damn singer in the whole wide world, I tell ya."

"I haven't heard of her."

"Really? She is a classic! She could put Sinatra to shame."

"Well, I like old music. Maybe I'll look for some of her songs on YouTube."

"So, what is India like?"

"Actually, I'm from Canada."

"Really? You must have been to India before though. Is it as hot as it is here? I'll bet!"

"Well, I've been there a couple of times, and it could get pretty hot..."

"Are you an arts student? Most of the young people here are students."

"No, I'm not a student. But I'm going to be staying with a friend, he is a student..."

"He must go to the art school. What does he study?"

"I...don't remember."

"Really? How well do you know him? How did you meet him?"

"I met him online."

"Really? Well, anyways, here's the nanny room. Let me know if you need anything. We'll be serving wine and desserts a few hours from now. If you want to come down and try some, I won't say anything." He winked.

"A little cake couldn't hurt," I remarked. Thank you."

*

As soon as the owner left, I threw my things on the canopy bed and hopped into a shower. I may have been in the most price-sensitive room in the house, the room that had once belonged to a rich family's nanny, but it was still quite extravagant. The bedroom featured a lofty bed, two fireplaces, and a large window with a killer view of the courtyard. Old oil paintings decorated the red brick walls.

I washed the sticky, dusty sweat off my hair and body. In slow-paced Savannah, I took the longest, most luxurious shower that I had throughout my entire journey—possibly my entire life. I must have spent at least an hour in that shower, scrubbing every inch of myself until the hot water ran cold. Then I lathered my whole body generously with a small bottle of hotel lotion.

I wrapped myself in a soft, thick towel and hopped into the queen-sized bed, feeling like a princess. I checked my email. There was a message from Keshav:

Hi Samita,

Thanks for sharing good food and conversation with Sachin and me, and telling us about that language-learning site. By the way, we've been listening to the audio version of the Gita, and will play at least a chapter a day when we cook dinner.

I trust you're well?

Come back anytime. You can even bring your parents. They'll take my room, you'll take the mattress, and I'll sleep on the couch.

We'll try your veg burger idea soon, and let you know how it goes!

Regards,

Keshav

I was happy to see that even though he had come to the West from India very recently and was proud of Indian culture—its language, food, and the practice of yoga—I had managed to share with him the most important of India's many jewels: *The Bhagavad Gita*. The book encompassed the true meaning of "yoga," which was to connect with the divine.

In actuality, *The Bhagavad Gita* is not simply a "cultural book" or a "religious book," but a timeless philosophical book that can help anybody, anywhere. It is not just for Indians. The philosophy of *The Bhagavad Gita* is universal and humanistic, which is part of what made the book such an excellent travel companion.

After all, they say that there is no difference between the Lord and his word.

I wrote Keshav back, thanking him for his hospitality. I let him know that I was safe in Savannah. Then I sent another quick message to the woman from the bus, and attached a few pictures of my journey. I called my parents.

And of course, I had a new text message waiting for me from an old friend: "Where r u now?"

"Georgia," I wrote back.

"OMG. Try not to get lynched!"

"Not funny, Latoya."

"Love u 2."

I got changed, which was hard to do since I was running out of clean clothes, and went downstairs to the parlor. A decadent cake sat atop a corner table, along with two bottles of wine. Some older couples were sitting on the couches and chairs around an empty fireplace. I realized that I was the only person in the B&B who had come alone, and who was under sixty.

"Hello there," an elderly black man greeted me. He had hooded, amber coloured eyes. "Where do you come from?"

"Canada. How about you?"

"Scarlett and I are from Atlanta. We come here almost every year on our anniversary," he said, introducing me to his white wife. She was old, but elegant and well-dressed, with a sense of regality about her.

Ha! And they're not even young! I wish Latoya was here to see this, I thought to myself. I made a mental note to tell her about it later, so she could eat her words about all those American stereotypes! But I never did remember, which was just as well. She would never have believed me.

I helped myself to a generous portion of cake. I looked around. I never drank at home, and hadn't had a drink since university. No one was watching. I knew that drinking was frowned upon, prohibited even, for people who wanted to develop spiritually. Still, out of curiosity, or perhaps just because I could, I poured myself a couple of tablespoons of red wine into a glass.

I brought the glass to my lips. The smell was foul!

I let the taste of the wine wet my lips. There was a reason people always asked, "What's your poison?" It was definitely an acquired taste. A taste I myself had acquired at one point in my life, out dancing on campus pub nights with Latoya.

I thought of all the times I had gone too far, and how I'd finally had my fill. I knew it was spiritually detrimental, but it was also physically detrimental, and it was something I never wanted to touch again. That part of my life was over, and I was glad for it.

I put down the glass, and enjoyed my cake by the grandfather clock.

*

I brought another slice of cake up to my room, and spent the rest of the evening on my little laptop, looking up other places I could stay and things I could do in the South.

Should I check out Atlanta? Orlando? New Orleans?

There was a knock at my door.

"Here's your turn down service," said the curly haired owner, handing me a couple of chocolates. "Everything alright? You feeling okay? Did you come down for a little wine? You can tell me."

70

Ah. It was then that I fully understood what he meant about "not saying anything" if I chose to have a little wine-and-cake binge.

"No, I didn't drink. But sir...I'm twenty-three."

"Really? Twenty-three? I thought you were about sixteen."

I smiled. "Thank you. I'll take that as a compliment. But actually, everything isn't totally alright. I'm running out of fresh clothes to wear. Do you know where I can find a Laundromat?"

"You can use our laundry room. Let's just not tell anyone about this. One of our maids strictly handles the laundry, and she can get pretty upset when anyone else messes with her business—including us!"

I highly doubted that was true. I had noticed that the secrecy thing was just a tactic that the owners used to build a rapport with their guests.

"Thank you. And don't worry. I won't tell anyone," I said, playing along.

*

Savannah capitalized on being a ghost town. Many businesses advertised haunted tours of historic mansions and cemeteries where there had been supernatural sightings. I thought it would be a cute, touristy experience to spend a night of indulgence in a "haunted" mansion, but come nightfall, I regretted the decision. In the dim moonlight, the oil portraits in the room looked positively menacing.

I texted Latoya.

"Can't sleep. Scared of ghosts."

What am I doing? She'll probably just make it worse, I thought.

After a few minutes, she texted back.

"Ghosts can't touch u."

"I'm in a really old mansion full of paintings of fallen Confederate soldiers," I wrote, egging her on.

"So? Those soldiers r D-E-A-D. Go to sleep!"

"<3"

"<3 u more."

When I needed her most, Latoya was a good friend. But despite her consolation, I fell into a late, uneasy sleep, keeping one eye open for forgotten phantoms. It was kind of ironic: I booked a night at a fancy B&B so that I could have a little bit of respite after days spent pounding city pavements and nights on shaky buses, but the idea had completely backfired.

The Bible Belt

I woke up super early and headed down to the laundry room to get a wash done before my host came to pick me up. There were many machines, most of them full with bed sheets, but I found an empty one, and stuffed it full of my clothes. I was surprised by how many I had—fresh shirts went quickly in the blistering July weather.

I went back upstairs to shower, where I noticed that the bug bite I had acquired on my arm the day before was now red and swollen.

After packing up, having breakfast, and checking out, I waited for my host in the parlor. He was a short, hefty redhead with sharp features. When he arrived, he shook my hand and helped me get my luggage into his hatchback.

"Hi, I'm Drew." He shook my hand firmly, looking me up and down through almond-shaped green eyes.

Drew was a chatty Northerner born in Boston. He told me about what an adjustment it was to move out of his parents' house to live alone in the Deep South.

"My friends come down to visit and they tell me 'dude, you have such a drawl now'...Do you hear it?"

"No, you sound like me. Do you ever miss home?"

"Oh yeah, but I really wanted to study fashion design. What do you do?"

I thought to myself for a moment.

"I'm a writer," I said.

God, that felt good.

"Wow, great. How do you like the South so far?" he inquired.

"I could get used to the rhythm around here."

"Oh, I know what you mean. In the city, getting anywhere took at least thirty minutes. Here, if a commute is any longer than thirty minutes, I'm not going!"

"No kidding. It takes about thirty minutes for me to walk across town."

"Yeah, that's about right," said Drew. "Hey, what do you want to do tonight? Go to a bar? Catch a movie?"

"I don't know...I'm pretty tired. To be honest, I don't drink. But I do like to dance."

An image of Drew holding my waist in a thinly lit club flashed across my mind, making my stomach turn.

Why did I tell him I like dancing?

"Oh okay, that's cool. By the way, I still have a guest staying at my house. He's catching a bus later this afternoon, so you'll get to meet him for a bit," Drew remarked nonchalantly.

"Cool."

Drew drove me to his artist's loft, which was, like Savannah itself, a mixture of the old and new. It had old-fashioned beaming, brick walls, and a real fireplace, contrasted against modern appliances and technology. The hardwood floor bore the marks of all the guests that had passed through the loft over the past hundred years.

A tall, freckly man in his early twenties sat on the couch that was soon to become my bed. He was packing up his things.

He looked up. "I'm Xander," he told me, revealing a subtle Dutch accent.

"Samita."

"I'll let you guys get acquainted. I have to go to school," Drew announced, patting me on the back. I felt a funny sensation in my stomach.

He handed me a key to his house. "Feel free to walk around and let yourself in whenever. I'll be back at five and we'll hang out then."

*

Xander and I chatted while he finished packing. Like me, he was on an almost month-long trip from a foreign country, but while my pace was starting to slow during the latter half of my journey, his was just picking up. I was going north to south, but he was going east to west; from sea to shining sea. His next stop was New Orleans.

"Exciting!" I commented. "So, what all is there to do in Savannah?"

"I was only here for two days and one night. Drew and I didn't do much. We went to a bar by the river. We met a nice man there who bought me a drink. People here are very friendly."

I nodded. "Okay, but Xander, this is an art town. There must be museums or galleries something."

"Ah!" said Xander, as he lifted a finger. "One moment."

He shuffled through his duffle bag.

"Drew gave me this," he divulged, handing me a crumpled piece of paper. I unfolded it.

"It's a bundle card to get into three attractions for less dollars...Is that proper English?"

"I understand. Hey, this is awesome! Let's do this!"

"You have it. I only have three hours or so."

"So you want to spend them in here? Come with me!"

Xander looked hesitant. I pulled out my map of Savannah from my purse. It was also already looking a little the worse for wear.

"Look. There's more than enough time to see at least one or two of these," I coaxed.

"Okay," he sighed. "Why not?"

He lifted his duffle bag over his shoulder and headed for the door. I grabbed my purse, slipped into my flip flops, and joined him.

We started with the Telfair Academy, which was an art museum almost side by side with the Jepson Center. We walked around the galleries for almost two hours, observing various oil paintings of old white dudes and fallen Confederate soldiers. Then, we made our way to the Jepson Center's modern art section. There was an exhibition on Howard Finster, an artist who had done cover art for R.E.M. and Talking Heads. It was by far the most bizarre art exhibit I've ever seen, and I still remember it like it was yesterday.

His art was downright creepy. He painted demons and torture scenarios, and wrote misspelled messages on several of his paintings condemning his audience's souls to eternal damnation for various unforgivable sins, such as homosexuality. I wondered if they were parody pieces, but I soon realized that his message was taken seriously by interpreters. He couldn't see his own hypocrisy, claiming to be a "man of light" while his mind was full of evil, judgement, and darkness—qualities he projected onto God.

"He's telling us, in very poor English, that we're all going to hell. And here's what's going to happen when we get there," I said, examining a depiction of Armageddon.

"Fascinating!" Xander exclaimed, as he inspected Finster's art. "We don't really have these evangelists in Europe."

"None at all?"

"It's very, *very* rare. His mind is just so interesting to me."

"Interesting to you; terrifying to me. Maybe we should check out another gallery."

"I'd like to stay for a bit," Xander countered, gazing at one of Finster's creepier creations. His eyes were somewhere else, in Howard Finster's alternate universe.

"We should go. To be honest, this is making me a little uncomfortable," I pressed.

"That's what good art does," he responded.

I glared at him.

"Oh, alright, fine," he said with a sigh. "I must admit, this isn't the kind of work I would display myself if I was an artist. I'm just *fascinated* that someone thinks this way and is willing to broadcast their views to the world like that."

"Do you want to go to the Owens-Thomas house?" I suggested.

"I'm too hungry to walk around anymore. I should eat before I go."

"Okay. There's a cafe here at the gallery."

"Out of my budget."

"Then let's find a grocer. I could also stock up on some snacks."

As we wandered around a bit I asked him about how he liked the Amtrak. He had bought a monthly train pass and was using it go wherever he wanted. His only stipulation was that he had to be on the other side of the continental United States at a specific time to get his return ticket.

"I'm doing something similar, except I'm going by bus," I said.

"It's good. The only problem is the homeless at the stations. I cannot say no."

"Are you serious? I have the same problem whenever I wait for the Greyhound!" I confessed.

"There was this time...I was in one of the Carolinas, and someone told me a very sad story. Even though a part of me was asking myself, 'what are you doing?' I couldn't help but give him a dollar."

"I think I met the exact same person," I said.

Xander and I found a convenience store after a couple of blocks. He bought a loaf of bread and a gross looking can of processed meat, and I bought a container of nuts for a fraction of what they would have cost in Canada.

We sat in one of Savannah's many square parks while we ate our snacks. I was enjoying another hot, muggy day in a shockingly quiet town full of green spaces. It was a welcome change from DC and NYC.

"Don't you just love the South? These nuts were a steal! Everything here is so cheap," I stated.

Xander shook his head as he looked down at the sandwich he had just put together. "That's not a good thing. American bread will never compare to what we have in European bakeries."

"Check the label—at least here it's fortified with vitamins!" I retorted.

Xander shrugged. "Well, I do find this country interesting. That's for sure. Look at the characters."

"Do you think that artist was serious?"

"*He* sure is," said Xander. He gestured subtly at an elderly picketer sporting a fedora and a white suit.

The man was standing in the middle of the park, holding a sign that said "SATAN IS VERY BAD."

"Not much to protest about. No one's arguing with him," I remarked.

Finster was either an insane person or an artistic genius. A disturbed, self-proclaimed "man of visions" or a marketing king with a small fan base that agreed with him and a wide audience of puzzled critics. Who knows? Maybe he was just a brilliant satirist, and he laughed at all of us on his way to the bank, scoring famous rock stars as clients.

"What are your thoughts on God?" Xander asked.

I showed him *The Bhagavad Gita*, which I was still carrying in my worn handbag.

"This is a philosophical guidebook," I told him. "It's a conversation between God and his friend."

"Is it in agreement with anything the artist says?"

"No. He was way off about a key issue: the soul."

I showed him some verses from Chapter Two.

For the soul there is neither birth nor death at any time. He has not come into being, does not come into being, and will not come into being. He is unborn, eternal, ever-existing and primeval. He is not slain when the body is slain.

The soul can never be cut to pieces by any weapon, nor burned by fire, nor moistened by water, nor withered by the wind.

—The Bhagavad Gita, 2.20, 2.23

"It is the body, not the soul, that feels pain. The soul is joyful and eternal just like our loving friend, mother, father, and creator, is joyful and eternal. God is not cruel or vengeful."

Xander nodded. "This is interesting, too. Although I don't understand...who is saying all of this?"

"Well, it's God, Xander."

"This book was spoken by God?"

"Yes, of course."

"That cannot be," said Xander. He looked bewildered.

"What do you mean?"

"God cannot be a person."

"Why not?"

Xander furrowed his dark, bushy brows. "I believe in a higher power," he said. He was speaking slowly, and carefully. "When I studied science in college, I just knew there had to be something beyond our world. The universe is so perfectly ordered. It was not put together by chance. The orbit of the planets, the orbit of the sun around the galaxy, even the smallest of atoms—it's all arranged so perfectly."

While many people with strongly held religious beliefs rejected science, Xander's faith was strengthened by it.

"Someone who could have done something so big couldn't have been a person like you or me. Why would God care about us, and bother to have conversations with us?" Xander continued.

"Let me just ask you two things. Would you 'bother' to make a perfectly ordered universe, and then throw it to the wind?"

"Well, no," Xander conceded. I could tell he was thinking hard.

"And if God isn't a person, then why are we? We are individuals, each with our own personality."

Xander nodded.

"I have my own path, and you have yours. We have our own karma to work out."

"I agree."

"How could God give us qualities He doesn't have himself?" I quizzed.

"I don't know!" bellowed Xander, running his fingers through his hair.

I could tell that I had got him thinking, so I didn't press further.

"Are there any rules I would have to follow to join this philosophy?" he asked me.

"If you are serious about your spirituality, the number one thing is to not do harm to other living beings, human or animal," I disclosed.

Xander looked down at his meat sandwich again. "I'm sorry," he whispered.

I wasn't sure whether or not he was apologizing to me, the dead animal, God, or himself.

"I think that Buddhism is a better fit for me," he continued. "There is no personal God for me to talk to, and I wouldn't have to follow any rules."

I wasn't sure why anyone wouldn't want to talk to God, but I told Xander that Lord Buddha was actually an avatar of Lord Krishna, who descended during a time of cruelty and impiety to spread the message of *ahimsa* (nonviolence) and curb animal slaughter.

"He did not reveal all that's in *The Bhagavad Gita* because he knew that people were not ready to develop a personal relationship with God. The first step was to soften their hearts with moralism, by encouraging them to stop killing. Spirituality is one step further than morality."

"I see...It's a good philosophy. Maybe I should become a vegetarian," Xander considered.

We walked back to Drew's place, where Xander brushed his teeth and picked up his bags. He gave me the discount card. There was still one final destination that we hadn't seen yet: the Owens-Thomas House.

"You take this," he said.

"Thank you."

"It was nice talking to you. Good luck with your travels." He shook my hand.

"You too."

Xander left.

*

I was on my laptop, settling into my couch/bed when Drew returned. I told him about my day with Xander, the art exhibit and the picketer.

Drew looked unsurprised. "You're in the Bible Belt now," he said casually.

"The what?"

"The stretch of land starting in Virginia and going down the coast to Texas."

"So that explains the biblical bus crooner."

Drew chucked. "Who?"

I told Drew about the episode that occurred during my bus ride down to Savannah.

"Yep. Nothing unusual about that."

I asked Drew what he wanted to have for dinner.

"As long as it's vegetarian, I'll make it for you," I told him.

"You pick," he decided. "I like to try out food from different cultures. When someone's willing to cook, I let them."

"Okay. I'll make you some rice and beans."

"Cuban food! I think I have that stuff...We might have to go to the grocery store."

"Do you have spices?"

"I have pepper."

"Cayenne pepper?"

"Never heard of it. I think I should just take you to the store."

Drew drove me to a huge grocery store, several times larger than the convenience store I visited earlier with Xander. He parked at the edge of the generous parking lot, with room to spare on both sides.

"Oh, that's so Georgia," he said, pointing at the bumper sticker on the van in front of us.

It read, "Gun control is being able to hit your target."

Drew bought me whatever I wanted at the grocery store. I picked up a bag of dried pasta and some fresh tomatoes, lots of vegetables for soup, lots of fruit, a bag of lentil, flour, sugar, baking powder, baking soda for cake making, and some key spices: cayenne pepper and curry powder.

"Wow, you guys have Jamaican curry powder here. That's the good stuff," I told him.

Drew shrugged. "Whatever you want."

Afterward, he drove me to a Wal-Mart supercenter to stock up on toiletries. I looked for an eye care centre where I could get my glasses repaired, but there wasn't one.

"Check this out!" said Drew, showing me a bottle of purple hand soap.

Directions: Use to wash hands as you would any hand soap.

He put it into the cart.

*

I cooked some rice and black beans for dinner, seasoning the beans with cayenne and curry for "zap." Drew loved it.

"I'll help you clean up," I suggested.

"No, you have a seat. The person who cooked shouldn't be the one who does the dishes. House rules," he declared.

"Okay," I said, feeling grateful. It was about ten-thirty at night, and I could barely keep my head up to finish eating dinner.

"So you're staying a couple of nights?"

"Yeah, I think so. I didn't book my next bus ticket yet because I'm not quite sure where to go from here," I admitted.

"I think three days or so is perfect for Savannah. Whatever you want to do, I'm fine with it. I don't have another guest lined up for weeks."

"Thank you."

"So do you want to watch a movie tonight? I could put something on and we can just stay in," proposed Drew.

"I'm too tired. Rain check?"

"Okay," said Drew. "See you tomorrow."

"Goodnight."

It was true that I was way too tired for a movie, but it wasn't the whole truth. I wasn't physically attracted to Drew, but I felt a peculiar, uncomfortable tension around him. The thought of sitting beside him on a couch for two hours, sharing a bowl of popcorn was enough to make me cringe and break out into a cold sweat. Why did I feel this way? I had no such sensations around Keshav and Sachin.

I brushed my teeth, brushed off the feelings, and went to sleep as soon as I lay down on that big comfy couch. Since I began my travels, my sleeps had been characterized by either jostling dozes or deep comas, but for the first time, I had a vivid dream.

*

I looked up, and Drew was standing on the other side of the couch, towering over me.

"Do you want me to touch you?"

"Well, it has been a while."

He stepped toward me, now sitting beside me as I lay on the couch.

"A while since what?"

"Since I felt the touch of a man."

"Like this?"

He ran his hands up my body, squeezing my breasts.

"What do you want me to do?"

"Undress me..." I whispered.

*

I woke up from the salacious dream, in a cold sweat.

Shit.

For him who has conquered the mind, the mind is the best of friends; but for one who has failed to do so, his mind will remain the greatest enemy.

—The Bhagavad Gita, 6.6

A Haunting History

Drew and I sat at his kitchen table, having a peanut butter toast breakfast.

"What are you planning to do today?" he quizzed.

"What do you think of those haunted tours of the town?"

"Those are overrated."

When Drew left, I took a shower, and washed all thoughts of last night's dream down the drain. I changed out of my pyjama shorts and into a light, flowery sundress. I stocked my purse with my map, water, nuts, granola bars, my journal, and *The Bhagavad Gita*. I decided to go to Savannah's civil rights museum, and then head over to the Owens-Thomas house with the coupon Xander gave me.

*

A private tour guide was giving a tour of the museum when I arrived as part of a package deal. I paid the low entry fee into the museum, and then listened in as the guide led his small group.

He informed the group that Savannah had a relatively nonviolent civil rights movement. He mentioned which streets were for blacks/Asians (MLK Blvd.) and which ones were whites-only. Then there were certain individual establishments that were a grey area.

"Levy's Diner only served whites, but blacks were allowed to work in the back."

I pulled out my map and tried to picture how the town was segregated decades ago.

The museum had old public water coolers made of tin. One was labelled "coloured water," a phrase which has a completely different meaning in modern society.

One of the things that surprised me most was the section about women who opposed the civil rights movement. The museum informed that many white women joined counter civil rights protests, carrying signs that said "what about OUR rights?" I was taken aback by the short-sightedness of women who felt that only one disadvantaged group could be given equal rights. They felt threatened, falsely reasoning that if blacks had rights, women never would.

Segregation was a result of slavery. From what I'd gathered from Smithsonian exhibits, it wasn't uncommon for slave owners to have mixed children, and since people were property, consent was never a factor. Knowing that, I thought it was extremely naive that these female protestors genuinely thought that people who oppressed blacks—the same people who probably yearned for "the good old days"—would be so in favour of feminism.

I perused the postcard stands in the gift shop, wondering if I should buy them for friends or relatives. It was a cute, quaint thing to do, and I was in a cute, quaint town. I looked at the price tag: they were four dollars each—*no thanks*.

"Hello, ma'am," the cashier behind the counter greeted. He was a thirty-something black man, about five-foot-five, with a slender frame and plump, reddish brown lips. "What did you think of the museum?"

"It was good," I said, revealing my accent.

"Where you from, honey? Up north, aren't you? I bet you're a city girl."

"Mhmm," I responded vaguely.

"Take as many postcards as you want for your folks back home. No charge."

"Thanks," I said, grabbing one.

"You got more than one friend?"

"Okay." I smiled, selecting two more.

"You know, I think I got something for you in the back. Wait here," he instructed.

He came out after a minute and handed me a book on Gullah culture. "Our forefathers and mothers contributed to make this country what it is today. You need to learn your history—*our* history."

I looked over the book, and slowly it hit me: *He thinks I'm black. And American.*

I did not correct him.

"I thank the Lord we don't live in those times. Sometimes I feel like putting on that KKK uniform we have on displa. You see it?"

"Yeah. Why would you do that?"

"Just to walk around with it, see what kind of reactions I'd get." He continued, "I'd get to find out how people really feel."

"I still think women have it worse," I contended. "I was shocked to see that ridiculous photograph of the female anti-civil rights protestors. Sometimes I think no one in society suffers more than women, and to wish that on others is just beyond me."

"What you mean?" he probed.

A couple of other people in the gift shop turned and gave me a funny look, then went back to looking at the shelves while they listened in.

"Well, who's the President of the United States? And it's not like there's ever been a female one," I said, worried that I was sounding a little too glib.

The man thought for a moment.

"You're right," he concurred. "Even us brothers are to blame for that. The way I seen some men down on MLK Boulevard holler at women...And of course, the internet, the media, and having all this pornography available everywhere don't help none."

I was glad that he wasn't offended by what I said.

"Hey, if you ever wanna talk more on this, let me give you our card," he said, handing me his business card. He scrawled his cell number on the back. "We could even talk over some dinner."

"Thanks. Well, see you around."

I never called, but to this day, I've still kept the postcards, book, and even the business card as mementos.

*

The palatial Owens-Thomas house, almost two hundred years old at the time, was undergoing significant renovations.

"A house as old as this ain't never done with renovations," admitted the delicate, blonde, wispy-haired guide.

She led us through the old mansion, which was the first house in America to have indoor plumbing, and she told us about the significance of each thoughtfully designed room according to social customs.

"This here is the guest dining room, and over *here* is the regular dining room. You would never use this room when you were entertaining, unless of course you were low class or just plain insulting someone."

90

An indoor bridge joined different sections of the upper floor. The guide helped one of the frightened younger guests cross the bridge.

"Don't worry honey. This house is built solid! The walls are much thicker than many built according to today's codes," she said soothingly. Then she gestured at a picture of the lady of the house, hung on an intricately detailed frame. "Bless her heart. She wasn't much of a looker."

The group chortled.

"It ain't such a bad thing. Back in those days, many high-class women wouldn't marry. It meant giving all their earnings to a man's name."

She took us into the mansion's slave quarters, which were substantially different from the regal main building. Seeing the paraphernalia of long-gone residents of the past was sobering—part of why I enjoy museums so much. The walls of the quarters were still painted with a cracked coat of blue. It was a spiritual tradition with African roots, meant to protect the room from "haints."

"Probably accounts for why this is the only house in Savannah that ain't haunted!" joked our guide.

*

I let myself into Drew's place. He was already home, directing a handyman as he finished fixing the air conditioning.

"This little lady here your girlfriend?" he asked Drew, as I walked in.

"No, she's just a friend. Visiting from Canada."

"Oh," said the handyman, moving on. "Where's that other guy who used to live here, the one with the black hair?"

91

"He moved out."

"How your studies going?"

*

"Sorry about him," said Drew, closing the door after the handyman finished up. "He's insanely chatty."

"I don't mind."

I headed over to the kitchen to begin whipping up some pasta for dinner.

"So how was the museum?"

"I went to two, actually. They were good. I'm glad times have changed so much though."

"Don't be so gullible! There are still people out there who think that way," he asserted. "More who don't than do—but you can't be too careful."

"Xander was telling me about how nice that people are."

"He's so naive. If he told you about that guy from the bar, he wasn't nice; he was just hitting on him."

I laughed. "Really?"

"Samita, I think I need to give you a lesson in Southern etiquette."

"Ooh, exciting!" I said, retrieving the tomatoes from the fridge. "Great. Teach me what I need to know before I get a chance to mess up."

"Alright. When you buy something, *always* hand the cashier the money—never just put it on the counter."

"Okay. Why not?"

"Some people can be sensitive about it. I had a friend who had moved here recently. He put money on the counter and tried to take his change back from the cashier's hand. She said, 'No! You put it on the counter, you pick it up from the counter!'"

"He was white and she was black?"

"Not really. He was Cuban. He was so confused."

"Don't put money on the counter—gotcha."

I boiled the chopped tomatoes in a pot with some fried spices. In another pot, I cooked the pasta noodles.

"Race issues still exist. Not to me though. In DC, nobody cares about that stuff."

"*Nobody?*"

"Well, not my family. They told me I can date whoever I want. Are your parents like that? Or are you going to do that whole arranged marriage thing?"

"No arranged marriage for me."

"What about dating non-Indians? I heard some parents freak out about that stuff."

"We'll see," I said nonchalantly, but I didn't like where the conversation was headed.

"I've dated interracially before. I don't even really like blondes or redheads. I much prefer exotic brunettes."

"Oh?" I said coolly.

"Definitely. What about you? Do you have a type?"

"Tall, dark, and handsome," I listed.

Drew fell silent, and I finished cooking without further conversation.

I served us dinner at the table.

"This is your first time couch surfing, right?"

"Yes. How about you? Have you ever been on the receiving end of a couch?" I inquired.

"Lots of times during my Eurotrip. I stayed with many beautiful European girls...but I would never make a move on a couch surfer. It's just totally inappropriate."

"I agree."

Deep Exploration

I was starting to fall in love with Savannah. The haunting trees, the sweet accents, the peaceful quietness. With Drew's strange vibes, a little voice in my head was telling me to move on...but the part of me that wanted to stay was more overwhelming.

I took a walk along River Street, a modern, touristy area that followed the Savannah River. It was lined with gift shops, pubs, and creameries along cobblestone roads. It was Savannah in the twenty-first century. I wore shorts and a loose tee, and I wasn't too warm. If anything, when the breeze hit, I felt a little bit chilly. I was getting acclimatized.

Most of the shops sold beach clothes, sundresses, and artsy, kitschy things. Incense. Nose rings. Jewellery that changed colour based on body temperature or "mood."

I was wandering through a store that sold mala beads, Buddha figurines, and books on meditation. I was eyeing a black sundress with a bright pink and orange Paisley design.

"Are you a Buddhist?" I asked the owner.

"No, but I like that kind of stuff. Why do you ask?"

"I saw that you sell a lot of spiritual books and Buddha statues."

"I have the perfect gift for you!" he announced.

He disappeared momentarily, and then handed me some mala beads.

"Wow, cool. How much?"

"It's a *gift*, love."

"Thank you!" I said. I put it in my bag, picked up the black dress, and headed over to the change room.

The owner approached me again. "That would look great on you!"

"I wanted to try it on, but the door is locked."

"I'll get the key for you." He reached behind the counter. "So where are you visiting from?"

"Canada."

"Oh, cool! I moved here recently from Vermont with my girlfriend."

He handed me the key. I reached for it, but then he promptly withdrew it.

"Oh...what am I doing? Here, let me get the door for you. Sorry, I was just enamoured by your big, dark eyes. They go perfectly with that dress, by the way!"

"Okay...Thanks."

When I emerged from the change room, he was waiting nearby.

"Don't even bother taking that off!" he exclaimed. He got a sales bag. "Put your t-shirt in here, and just walk around the rest of the day in that dress. The bright colours really contrast against your brown skin and hair."

Wow, did he know how to sell a dress! He didn't have to work so hard; I had severely under packed, and was in dire need of new clothes. I wanted to buy that dress from the moment I set eyes on it.

"Sure, I love the dress. I'll take it."

He started to ring me up.

"By the way, I noticed that this mala only has ninety beads; it should have a hundred and eight."

"I'm so sorry...do you still want it?"

"Of course, it's a souvenir."

"Still...it isn't right. Let me call our supplier right away."

He handed me back my change and told me to wait while he phoned the supplier in front of me, asking them to send malas with the correct number of beads in the future.

"So you're a practicing Buddhist, I take it?" he questioned, once he got off the phone.

"No. I follow *sanatana dharma*, a non-sectarian path. Have you heard of *The Bhagavad Gita*?"

"No."

I handed him the book from my bag. "This is our philosophical book."

"That's so interesting. I'd love to read it someday."

I penned down the url for Vedabase, a website where the book could be read online, and handed him the post-it.

"You!" exclaimed another customer who had been observing our interaction. He was an older gentleman with a thick Indian accent. He pointed and headed toward me. "You Hindu? Hare Krishna?"

"How did you know?"

"Neck," he said, indicating my *tulsi* beads.

He told me that he had also never read the *Gita*. I wrote down another note with the Vedabase url, and handed it to him as well.

*

I went into a creamery and bought a fruity popsicle. Then I sat down by a flower bed, looking over at the river that led to the ocean, while I sucked on my sugar fix. Beside me there were some Chinese students studying together, and a fair-haired woman who bounced her strawberry blond grandson on her knee, holding him with one hand while she smoked a cigarette with the other. She bounced him to the rhythm of a middle-aged street musician with straw-like hair and a bulbous red nose.

"*Country roads, take me home, to the place, where I belong,*" he sang.

His voice was phenomenal. When he finished with John Denver, he sang "Sweet Home Alabama" and some other Skynyrd songs as he strummed his guitar. The calming music, combined with the breeze from the river flowing into the Atlantic was so relaxing that I didn't know if I would ever be able to get up.

A person who is not disturbed by the incessant flow of desires—that enter like rivers into the ocean, which is ever being filled but is always still—can alone achieve peace, and not the man who strives to satisfy such desires.

—The Bhagavad Gita, 2.70

"Thank you for singing those songs. It was lovely," I told the man, when I finally gathered the gumption to awake from my reverie.

"No problem, dear," he said.

I gave him a dollar, and continued down the path, where I saw many spectacular monuments, such as the WWII monument, the African American monument, and The Waving Girl—a statue commemorating a young lady who had once greeted ships arriving at the harbour.

*

I was so relaxed that evening, my spirit completely imbibed with the Southern pace of life, that I wasn't able to cook. I chopped up some fruits and had a fruit salad dinner. Drew pan fried a burger, which produced the putrid aroma of burned flesh throughout the loft. He washed down his meal with a beer.

"I'm sorry. Hope the smell doesn't get to you too much."

"Whatever," I said with a shrug, but I swore to myself it wouldn't happen again. For the rest of my stay in Savannah, I cooked dinner every evening: pastas, curry dishes, cakes, and because we were in the South, okra vegetable soups.

*

Over the next few days, I continued to deeply explore.

I went to the First African Baptist Church, a landmark site due to it once being a stop along the Underground Railroad. It was also still a thriving church, where people attended every Sunday.

I went to the SCAD art school, and went through the gallery like a true patron of the arts. There were a lot of out-there fashion displays. I briefly wondered what Drew would think of them.

I visited Flannery O'Connor's former home. Then I strolled through the park nearby and made my way over to an enormous cathedral.

A mass was in session, and a big sign in front of the door proclaimed that tourists were strictly prohibited. I entered quietly and sat in the back; I was now a worshiper, not a tourist. My only regret about doing this was that I wasn't able to take any pictures,

99

which would have been rude and tacky, and blown my tourist cover. The immaculately decorated cathedral featured marble pillars with gold finishes, grandiose stained glass windows, and large murals on the upper walls, next to a ceiling painted to mimic the glistening stars in the night sky.

It was my first time at mass, and I wasn't sure what to do. I followed everyone's lead, standing and sitting on cue. Because I had figured that one taste of wine was enough for a vacation, I shook my neighbours' hands, wished them peace, and snuck out the back when the sermon was over.

I went antiquing. I strolled into some strange shops, one of them selling a substantial amount of Nazi paraphernalia and mammy figurines—a sharp contrast from the kitschy riverside stores I'd visited days before.

"DUKE FOR PRESIDENT: IT'S THE WHITE THING TO DO," declared a button labelled as a "racial activist" piece.

That's a euphemism if there ever was one, I thought to myself.

Outside of that shop, there was a parked car that was completely covered with shells, figurines, and bumper stickers. It looked undrivable, because even the windows were covered with stickers. On the roof of the car, the figurines were piled several inches high. I had never seen anything like it in my life.

"You'll go to hell, and I'll go to TEXAS" was written on a rear bumper sticker.

Passersby gawked at it from the sidewalk. It was truly a sight to behold.

"What a car!" a lady said to me.

"It sure is something," I said noncommittally.

"It's a beauty is what it is."

I also spent a fair amount of time sitting on the bench outside the courthouse while I journaled. Even when I had nothing planned, now that I was adjusted I liked being outside in the pleasant, boggy heat rather than sitting in Drew's ice cold, air conditioned loft.

Drew had told me that three days was more than enough to see all that I needed to see in Savannah, but I never ran out of things to do. Like most places on earth, Savannah had a dark past, but it also had a lot of good, and that was what struck me the most. I fell in love with the quirky, artsy town, its friendly people, its welcoming weather, and its blend of antiquity and modernity.

I could probably have spent the rest of my life in Savannah, but I knew that sooner or later, I had to move on. Drew's comments and questions were becoming increasingly alarming. Had I ever had a one-night stand? What age did I think people usually lost their virginities in Canada? Would I ever consider being with another woman?

I didn't think he was a bad person. At the end of the day, Drew and I were both wanderers, just trying to get the most out of life. We were not so different.

The Supreme Lord is situated in everyone's heart, O Arjuna, and is directing the wanderings of all living entities, who are seated as on a machine, made of the material energy.

—The Bhagavad Gita, 18.61

I doubted that Drew knew how he was coming across, but it was clear that my time in this charming, quiet haven had run out. It was time for me to continue my journey somewhere else.

*

101

On my last day in Savannah, Drew drove me to the beach. We both had our bathing suits under our clothes, but I couldn't bear to disrobe from my new black sundress in front of him, so I went in the water fully clothed. Drew removed his shirt. His belly protruded, unable to be contained by his swimming trunks.

A year ago, on the coast of Ghana, I had taken a dip on the other side of the Atlantic. That was the last time I had been to a beach. Here I was again, bathing in that same ocean, except I was on the other side.

A large white bird took a sharp dive and grazed the water, took a gulp into its drooping beak, and flew off.

"Whoa. Was that a pelican?"

"Yep. That's nothing. I've seen dolphins here."

"So jealous," I said.

We walked along the shore until Drew got tired. The feeling of the sand between my toes was amazing. I collected beautiful shells to keep as souvenirs.

Drew picked up a sand dollar.

"This place used to be full of these, but people keep taking them home and killing them."

He tossed it back into the water.

*

That night, Drew let me do a load of laundry at his place and then drove me to the bus station to catch a midnight bus to Miami, Florida. We left a little bit early because Drew felt bad that I never got to do that "haunted tour" that most tourists do, so he decided to give me a personal one in his van. When he was about halfway through, I told him to stop, relieved that I hadn't gone on a paid tour, which would have been much more thorough and terrifying.

We passed some various strange scenes during my final moments in Savannah. A man played golf on his front lawn, shirtless. Two people rolled a friend of theirs down the middle of the road with a swivel chair.

"There isn't much to do here at night," Drew confessed.

He went into the station with me to make sure that I got a spot on the bus. I paid for the ticket, but realized my faux-pas a moment too late.

"Is it okay that I put my money on the counter?"

"You're fine," said Drew, smiling.

The cashier took no offense, and handed me a ticket.

"Well, I parked illegally, so I should be off. You're okay to wait alone?"

"Of course. Thanks for everything."

Drew hugged me goodbye, and I hugged him back.

No one talked to me at the station, and soon enough, the bus arrived.

Don't Be Scared

At this point in my journey, I had been through a lot. I had dealt with aggressive beggars, long periods without rest, harsh weather conditions, and I had almost fainted twice. But I was markedly less nervous than I was when I had begun. I had learned to fend off beggars (don't say no, just don't give them money—a fruit, a bar, or even a stick of gum will do). I was now well-rested after the healing touch of my new favourite town, I was well adjusted to the heat, and I had come up with a few precautions against light-headedness (eat often, and don't skimp on sugar). I could feel the fear and anxiety that had plagued me all my life fading away.

In this endeavor there is no loss or diminution, and a little advancement on this path can protect one from the most dangerous type of fear.

O son of Kuntī, declare it boldly that My devotee never perishes.

—The Bhagavad Gita, 2.40, 9.31

A beautiful woman with big blue eyes and Lady Godiva blonde hair sat in front of me, giving directions to someone on her cell phone so they could pick her up at the bus stop.

"Then you go straight," she directed, pronouncing "straight" to rhyme with "Sprite."

Most people were either on their phones or asleep. I tried my best to fall asleep, but the AC on the bus was so high, and I was shivering to the bone. I walked over to the bus driver.

"Excuse me, can you turn the AC down?"

"It's as high as it will go, ma'am."

"No, can you make it lower?"

"*Lower?* I can definitely do that!"

As I walked back to my seat, a man made a kissing sound at me. I ignored him, sat down, and went on my little laptop, Googling things to do in my final destination of Florida.

"*Pssst! Pssst!*" he called out to me. "You got a mother and a father?"

What?

I knew something was different about Miami because I was bombarded with Couchsurfing.org messages from males with pictureless profiles, inviting me to stay in their houses without me even sending out any requests or posting on any message boards. I decided to forgo even looking for a couch to sleep on, and to spring for a room in one of the city's many hostels.

I looked into the prices, and they were dirt cheap, with some rooms for less than ten dollars a night. I could have even stayed in a hotel for as little as twenty or twenty-five dollars.

"Great place to party!" said virtually every review of every hotel and hostel.

What was I getting myself into?

I wasn't sure, but I was excited to find out.

I felt rough, dirty fingers run from my scalp down my hair. I looked up, and it was him. He walked down the aisle to the washroom, and tried to touch me again on the way up.

Gross! And I had just washed my hair, too!

Infuriated, I marched to the back of the bus and sat with another group of travellers.

"Is he bothering you?" pressed a young black man with a goatee and petite facial features.

I nodded. "He asked me if I had any parents."

The group howled with laughter.

"Don't worry. He won't mess with you," he assured me. "I'm Ericson."

"Samita."

In Orlando, we unloaded. The man approached me when I was with Ericson and the gang and offered me a bag of peanuts. I said no.

"You from Florida?" he asked me. He pronounced it "Flo-ree-da."

"Get lost!" screeched one of the girls in the group.

He continued on his way, boarding at another platform.

"So glad he's not coming to Miami," I confided to my new friends.

Ericson and I chatted about politics. He was an ardent Republican. I told him about how I'd first heard about Obama winning the election.

"I was living in a university dorm at the time. It was late at night and I was asleep. All the guys in the dorm room started running down the halls, banging on all the doors and yelling 'OBAMA!'"

"Whoa!"

"I actually don't think I've ever met a Canadian who didn't want him to win."

"Well, you just met a Texan who didn't. I voted for Romney."

"Why?"

"He had the better campaign. Too bad Palin was the VP candidate. With Condoleezza Rice, he may have won."

When we got back on the bus, I snacked on some tapioca pudding I had brought from Canada while I took shots of the picturesque, swampy scenery of rural Florida. Ericson didn't know what tapioca was, so I gave him an extra plastic cup I had in my backpack.

I told him I was a vegetarian, and he asked me what I would do if I was stuck on a vegetation-free desert island with nothing to eat but other animals.

"I'd starve to death," I told him.

"I admire your conviction. Most vegetarians cave when I ask them that."

"Glad you don't think I'm crazy."

"That's not crazy. Now taking pictures of grass on the other hand…"

"Oh, but look at the beautiful grass! I haven't seen anything like this in Canada."

"Welcome to the swamp. You got those in Canada?"

"There's a park in Ontario called Point Peele, the southernmost part of Canada. It's a beautiful marshland."

"Beautiful? You must really love nature."

"I do. And your country is just full of so much beauty. You have deserts, forests, marshes…everything. Maybe on a future trip I'll even get to see the Grand Canyon."

"That hole in the ground? I think you might just love America more than I do!"

Before we parted ways at the Miami bus terminal, we added each other on Facebook.

"Let's see what other strange shots you'll take," he said.

"Don't worry. I'll post them all."

*

I walked out of the bus terminal and onto a corner, where I could catch a city bus across the bridge to Miami Beach. I wasn't even tired—I had gotten used to pulling all-nighters on bus trips—but I was still in for a shock when I stepped outside.

I hadn't anticipated such scorching heat. I had been cold on the bus, but I couldn't bear to have my sweater on for more than a second once I left the station. I took it off and tied it around my waist.

While I had gotten used to the heat in the humid, overcast town of Savannah, the Miami sun beat down relentlessly on my skin. Everyone around me was either tanned or just burned. Many men wandered around without shirts, and some without even shoes. It was not uncommon to see the "305" area code tattooed on a bronzed arm.

I boarded the bus, and as usual, struggled to find change.

When were city buses going to start accepting plastic?

The driver shook her rounded head, and her beaded braids dangled. "Forget about it. Just sit down."

I sat near the front of the bus, determined not to miss my stop. There was a plaque by the window beside it. The first seat of every bus in Miami was dedicated to Rosa Parks.

I had a map of Miami out in front of me that I printed when I was in Drew's house, and I was trying to follow along with the route as I craned my neck to read the street signs. Clad in baggy sweat pants for a comfy overnight journey, I was much more covered than anyone else. I couldn't have looked like more of a conspicuous tourist if I tried.

When the bus stopped, an older man got out a pencil and scrawled his number on the side of my map before he got off.

"Call me when you get settled. We'll go for a walk on the beach!" he said, before he got off.

I was so bemused, I didn't even respond. *Why had he done that?*

As he got off, two brothers boarded the bus. One looked like a teenager, the other in his early twenties. They sat beside me, and asked me what felt like hundreds of questions. Where was I from? What brought me to Miami? What kind of music did I like? Had I heard of their country, Puerto Rico? What did I do for a living? Where was I staying?

When I tried to answer the last question, I stammered a little. I had my map out in front of me, but I wasn't entirely sure where to get off and how far I would have to walk. They leered over the map, and the bus driver cut in.

"Oh, that hostel isn't on that street. You wrote it down wrong. It's on tenth."

"Really? I could have sworn..."

"—Don't worry. I'll get you there."

When the boys got off, the driver spoke to me.

"Look honey, I can tell you're a nice person. That's why I cut you a break on the fare. First time in Miami?"

"Is it that obvious?"

"To me and anyone else in a ten-mile radius. I've lived here for four years, and the things I've seen and heard in that time...You have to be careful."

I could tell that she was genuinely trying to look out for me, and I wanted to hear her insight.

"What do you advise?" I asked her.

"I know exactly where you're going, and I'll tell you when to get off. You had the address right, but I threw those boys off for you. They could have showed up at your hostel, asked for you, and no one would think twice of it. Before anyone had caught wind, you'd be gone. Stranger things have happened."

My jaw dropped.

"Hey—I said to be careful, not scared. Have fun. Enjoy Miami. When you get off, go straight into your hostel and make friends. With *girls*. I can see that you're a friendly person. You just need to open up to the right people, especially in a place like this. Once you make your group of friends, take them *everywhere*."

I nodded.

"Oh, I scared you! Don't be scared!" she said again, her beads jangling.

Where was that fearlessness I had channelled just a day before?

The 305

I walked to the hostel.

Make friends with girls. Take them everywhere.

Make friends with girls. Take them everywhere.

I heeded the bus driver's words, making them my new mantra.

I checked in to my room, which I was sharing with eight other women. I booked it for three nights. When I went in to drop off my stuff, no one was in the room.

Bags with wet bikinis and sandy clothes were strewn everywhere. Even the floor was full of sand.

I left my stuff in the room and went down to the main floor with just my handbag. A tall young woman with a pixie cut was typing away at her laptop.

"Hi, I'm Samita!" I said to her.

"I'm Eva," she replied curtly. "Well, take care!"

I was dismissed. I decided to try again later at night, when more people might be in.

"Can you point me to the beach?" I asked the two Norwegian men behind the counter, who had checked me in just five minutes before.

"Yes. You go outside, and you turn left. Keep going for about thirty seconds."

"Awesome, thanks."

I sat on the beach with my journal and my *Gita*, while people around me sat on the shore with cans of beer and bottles of liquor. Couples kissed in the water. I sat by myself, admiring the wonderful, terrible, beautiful, and deadly ocean.

...Of bodies of water I am the ocean.

—The Bhagavad Gita, 10.24

I had nothing to fear, because the most powerful person in the world, the Supreme Lord Krishna, was my friend. I knew that sooner or later, he'd send along some other companions for me too.

I left my books and towel by the shore and walked into the waters, until I was completely submerged. Then I returned to the shore, and was dry within fifteen minutes. My hair smelled like salt. I had been so desperate to wash it after that assault on the bus, but I no longer cared to. I liked the salty texture, and did not shower until the next morning.

I went back to the hostel at night, but it was still empty. When I woke up the next morning, there were a couple of ladies in the room with me, clearly in a deep sleep. I wondered how I would make friends during the final days of my travels. I thought that maybe this wasn't my place, and it was time to pack up and head somewhere else for a while, like Louisiana, or even Texas. I had almost two weeks, so there was still time to do so, if I really wanted to. As long as I was back in time for my flight, I could do whatever I wanted.

I showered, washing the sea salt out of my hair and off my skin. It must have had some therapeutic effects, because my giant Georgian bug bite was now just a dried scab. It flaked off in the shower, leaving a small white scar that would remain on my arm for another year. I actually cherished the scar because every time I looked down at it, I was reminded of my journey.

Amazingly, my New York manicure was still intact.

I sent a text to Latoya, informing her of my whereabouts.

"A hostel?! Do you WANT your kidneys stolen?"

"Thanks for your warm wishes. I'll try to have a good time."

*

Over the next couple of days, I explored Miami alone. I took twenty-five cent bus rides up and down South Beach, I went to grocery stores and stocked up on fruits, snagged some SPF one hundred at Walgreens, and spent loads of time on the beach. I couldn't really find much touristy things to do. Miami was known for its nightlife, not its attractions. I was getting bored. Everyone was out during the day, and the girls seemed unfriendly at night.

On my last night at the hostel, I booked a tour to the Everglades for the next morning. It was a little pricey, but at this point I had reasoned that this would probably be my one and only time in Miami, and my one and only chance to see the Everglades. This was the final shot: if I still wasn't happy with Miami by the next day, I'd move along to another city.

Boys, the Beach, and Female Friendships

I sat by myself as I finished the hostel's chocolate chip pancake breakfast, and then I walked outside to wait for the tour bus to pick me up in front of the building. Another girl was waiting beside me. She was a slim, tall blonde with dark roots and a creamy complexion.

"Are you waiting for the bus to the Everglades?"

"Yes," she said, in a European accent. "Are you also from the hostel?"

"Yep."

"Maybe we should stick together," she suggested. "I'm Rasa."

"Samita."

Rasa and I sat together on the bus. She told me that she had come to America as an au-pair nanny, and her stay in Miami was part of a last hurrah before she would have to return to Lithuania.

"Lithuania. It's in Europe, near the—"

I nodded.

"Oh you know? It's a surprise! What else you know of my country?"

"Not too much."

"It isn't very good. No high-rise, no choice of job, no choice of men...you understand what I'm saying?"

"I think so."

"Lithuania all blond, blond, blond...I want a handsome black man. Like you have here in America."

We both giggled.

Once we reached the Everglades, we boarded a noisy airboat, driven by a sunburned gentleman with a beard and a mullet.

Even with the burning bright sun, the water was a mysterious shade of dark brown, almost black. The murky, grassy water was filled with water lilies, between which alligators exposed their fierce heads.

"Y'all are lucky. Earlier morning crowd ain't seen but one gator!" the driver shouted.

This job had to be hard on the ears.

A turtle the size of a car tire emerged from the water, swimming freely between the grass blades.

"I 'on know about you city folk, but out here we call those a delicious soup!" he exclaimed.

We had some time to walk around the park grounds and explore the gift shop before the tour arrived. Outside of the store, alligator corpses were propped up on plastic lawn chairs and decked out in jeans, plaid farmer's shirt, and baseball caps. The store was full of cans of alligator meat on one side, and shellacked adult and baby alligator heads. I thought about how strange it was that people would buy these body parts as folksy souvenirs, thinking of them as sculptures rather than as the heads of dead parents and children that were once living, wild and free in the picturesque Everglades. I wondered how many alligators were hunted every year, or even every day?

I hoped that in the future, the Everglades wouldn't become barren.

Rasa and I walked around the park and took pictures under the exotic trees.

"So nice to have someone to take picture. Before, I asked strangers," she confessed.

"Me too."

Outside, one of the employees was letting whoever wanted take pictures holding a muzzled baby alligator. Rasa and I both posed for the pics, but I felt kind of guilty about it because the alligator looked so grumpy.

"*Hola*! You guys got *five* minutes!" shouted our bus driver.

We hurried back to the gift shop, bought some popsicles, and boarded the bus. Rasa bought a fudgsicle, and I bought a strawberry ice cream cone with sprinkles on top.

"Interesting choice!" Rasa chuckled.

We got back to our South Beach hostel in what felt like the blink of an eye, and it was still before noon.

"What to do now?" Rasa asked.

"I don't really know what all there is to do here, aside from lie on the beach."

"Ah...I have something to show you."

Under the blazing sun, Rasa and I walked for miles. When we passed Ocean Drive, drinks in martini glasses the size of my face lined restaurant windows, while waitresses greeted us and offered us these drinks for ten dollars if we came inside. Shirtless promoters invited us to parties in Mansion or LIV, if we would just give them a small two-to-five dollar "reservation" fee.

As we continued away from the South Beach frenzy, flashy convertibles whizzed by the palm tree-lined roads, painted garish neon colours. Even some of the pickup trucks had a coat of hot pink or highlighter yellow on them, topped off with ocean wave and seashell murals. Walking around Miami felt like being in an alternate reality.

Rasa led me to the Holocaust Memorial, and we walked around the botanical gardens, where we saw white storks and wild lizards. It was a strangely serene environment, and felt out of place in a city like Miami. Rasa wanted to walk back to our hostel, but I was feeling tired. We sat by the bus stop, where we waited for one of the city's twenty-five cent buses. Across the street, an obese man was holding a bag of Reese's Peanut Butter Cups. He popped them, one by one, into his mouth mechanically, as you would with a bag of potato chips. He threw the wrappers onto the ground, looking atrabilious.

"Is he okay?"

"I have seen many like him here...Crazy," Rasa commented.

"Why do you think that is?"

"It is shallow life: party, do some drugs, have some sex. No real connections with others."

The bus went down numerous side streets and residential neighbourhoods before passing flashy hotels, clubs and restaurants, and arriving close to our beachside destination. We had a comprehensive tour of South Beach. I wondered what it was like to live in a place like this, where people partied seven nights a week and the major attraction was a spectacular, ocean-side beach. Did it ever become boring? When, if ever, did the scenic beauty stop taking their breath away?

Rasa was getting hungry, so we walked to a grocery store and bought some pasta noodles, canned tomatoes, and cheese, before we went back to the hostel kitchen.

I started boiling the pasta noodles right away while Rasa ransacked the kitchen. It had several cooking supplies: pots, can openers, plates and forks, and even some spices. The electric can opener had seen better days, and neither Rasa nor I could get it to work.

"Let me at it!" interjected a short man with an Irish accent and a phallic shaved head. He had deep forehead creases, and a reddish tint to his skin. He began chatting up my new friend.

"What's your name? Rasa? I'm Connor. Where are you from? Oh...Lithuania? I heard they have the most beautiful women in the world..."

I snorted a little, but blew it off as a cough. It was easy enough to do over the sound of the boiling noodles.

"Well, I'll see you *chicas* later." Connor winked at Rasa.

"He was *so* hitting on you," I said to Rasa, the moment he left the room.

"No no...he was just telling the truth," she said seriously, handing me the open can of tomatoes.

I smiled, thanking Krishna for sending me a cool, funny new girlfriend.

*

That night, the hostel had arranged a pub crawl. Pub crawls aren't something I would typically be interested in. I considered them something I outgrew in my student days.

"Coming to Miami and no party...it is a sin," proclaimed Rasa.

I thought it was an interesting use of the word "sin," but I was easy to convince. There wasn't much else to do. Rasa said she would bring a couple of friends from her room, and we could all meet by the check-in at night and go together.

I sighed. "Sure. Why not? I'll see you tonight."

I went upstairs, brushed my hair, changed into my black sundress, and went back down to the lobby after nightfall.

The lobby and patio were crowded with other people from the hostel. Many had beers or coolers in their hands, chatting with newfound friends and practicing their dance moves. I stood on top of the stairs so I could get a good view. Connor was there. He waved at me, and I waved back before moving along. Among the din, I heard Rasa's mature, low-pitched voice. She was talking to two petite twenty-somethings with naturally bleach blonde hair. I waded through the crowd until I got to them.

*

Jeanie and Janet were sisters in their late twenties, travelling around the world from rural Belgium. After Miami and L.A., they were heading for Asia.

"Asia was Janet's idea, she's always wanted to visit. I said okay. This is the last bit of fun before we get serious," Jeanie told me while she nursed a beer.

She spoke slowly and thoughtfully. While Jeanie's English was good, I could see that she didn't speak it often, and most definitely not around her sister, although Janet spoke with much more fluency.

Jeanie was twenty-nine while Janet was twenty-six, but in her rhinestone studded tank and punky shorts, she looked like the younger of the two sisters.

"Janet has a boyfriend. When we return, she will marry him, and I will get serious with my job."

"And your boyfriend?"

"I'm single. There is one boy I'm casually seeing in Belgium," Jeanie revealed. "Not exclusively. One day I'll find real, passionate love." She took a sip of her beer. "Let me tell you something: I don't look twenty-nine, and I don't act twenty-nine. I like to work out, stay young, and have a good time."

"I'm single too. So is Rasa."

"Yes but we have each other. You see that girl over there?" Jeanie gestured at a dainty, bronzed brunette. "She's clubbing alone. How crazy!"

"She told you that?"

"She is from Spain. Doesn't speak one word of English, not that it matters here, where Spanish is more used."

"Hang on."

I approached the girl and asked her in Spanish if she was going dancing alone tonight.

"Her friends are coming, too," I relayed to Jeanie, who looked at me with astonishment.

"You speak Spanish!"

"A little, yes."

"Alright," said Jeanie decidedly. "Janet and I must take you everywhere we go."

Make friends with girls. Take them everywhere.

I shrugged. "That sounds fine to me."

*

The two Norwegian hotel staff were waiting for us outside. One had olive skin, hazel eyes, and an afro, while the other had straight, spiky, brown and blond hair. Apparently, one of them had connections to get us into Mansion for only fifteen dollars, but when he saw our outfits, he was in shock. Rasa was in her blue jeans. I was sporting flip flops. The other girls were dressed in similar casual, beachy outfits, and all of us were without makeup.

"Oh no. You will not get into Mansion like this," the staff member declared.

"Oh, is it my shoes?" I asked him.

"Yes. And your lack of makeup."

I told him about all of the people we met on the street who had offered to get us into night clubs for a couple of bucks.

"You can easily spend forty dollars to get into Mansion. Those people are crooks. They are only selling flyers and fake wristbands."

"If it's so expensive to get in, why do we have to dress up so much?" I asked, wondering what was in it for us.

"It's about the ego. You can tell people, '*Ooh, I got into Mansion*,' and they will tell you how hot you are," explained the staff.

"I don't get it."

He shook his head dismissively. "So ladies, are we going to change?" he proposed, addressing our group.

Some of the other girls nodded, but I confessed.

"This is the fanciest outfit I have."

"Alright then, we'll have to go to some more casual spots. Follow me."

*

121

I walked down the sidewalk with my beautiful blonde friends, the warm night-time breeze blowing against our hair. The only light came from the streetlights and the moon.

At night, South Beach looked stunning, but also scary. Drunken young men prowled the street. We walked past someone who was out cold on the pavement, fallen flat on their face. Dead drunk.

"Don't stop," the staff instructed us, so we kept going.

We made small talk with a few of the other guys and girls from the hostel. Most of the young men had their eyes fixated on Jeanie, who seemed to draw people in with her free-spirited personality. The quick-witted, somber Janet mostly kept to herself, keeping a watchful and protective eye over her older sister.

"She's popular with the men," I remarked to Rasa, gesturing at Jeanie.

"Mmmm, but what kind of men?" Rasa responded.

Though she hadn't heard us, Jeanie turned around immediately.

"Hey!" she called, linking arms with me. "You see that guy over there?"

With great disregard for smoothness, she made eyes at Connor, who was talking to the Spanish girl and palpably blowing her off.

"Yeah, I met him earlier. What about him?"

"Is he not the sexiest man alive?"

"Not really."

"I love studly, blond, blue-eyed men like that. Do you think he'll dance with me?"

"Oh, I don't know, Jeanie..." I said. "There's a million other guys who would love to, though."

"I don't like the blonds," chimed Rasa. "I much prefer a tall, dark, and handsome man. But everyone here is so tan, you can't tell who is black, who is white..."

After being immersed in the complicated racial politics of the South, it was refreshing to be around my new confidantes, who spoke so freely.

"What kind of men do you like, Samita?" Jeanie asked me.

I thought back to my last relationship with Shyam, the boy I left behind in Canada, and how tumultuously it had ended.

"I don't care what colour he is. I just want someone mature and drama-free. But still with a bit of a wild side."

"I will agree to that!" said Rasa.

We hopped from bar to bar. Jeanie danced with her sister Janet. A handsome black man bought a drink for Rasa, and she danced with him. I danced alone.

The bars were dirty, loud, and smelly, with flashing lights and broken bottles on the floor. The stench of cigarette smoke was overpowering. One of the hostel staff caught me holding my hand over my nose as I swayed to the beat.

"Where are you from?" he asked.

"Canada."

"It was hard for me at first, too. In Europe we don't smoke in the club. Especially not in the good ones."

I shimmied over to Rasa and tried to pose for some selfies with her, but none of them came out well. (This was just before the advent of the front-facing cell cam.)

"I'm sorry," I said, frowning as I scrolled through our pics together.

"For what? The bad music?"

I laughed. "I'll go ask the staff when we'll be heading back to the hostel."

Jeannie ran up to us, and there were tears in her eyes. Janet was close behind.

"Honey what's wrong?" I embraced Jeanie. Even her hair smelled like alcohol. "Did someone touch you? Tell me who it was!"

Jeanie shook her head vigorously. "I wish!" she moaned.

Rasa and I looked at her with confusion.

"It's Connor. He won't dance with me! He said he only wants a brunette!" Jeanie slurred.

I recalled his earlier encounter with Rasa.

"Oh, Jeanie that's bullshit."

"Then why won't he dance with me! He is the best looking guy I ever saw!"

Rasa and I exchanged a skeptical glance.

"He isn't, Jeanie. He looks like...well, he looks like a penis. *Definitely* nothing to cry over," I assured her.

Rasa stifled a laugh, but Jeanie still looked somber.

"Wait here. I'll be right back."

I went over to the hostel staff, who were standing by the bar, supervising our group.

"Maybe we should all head back soon," I suggested.

"We usually do."

"How much longer are we going to be staying for?"

"As long as people want. We don't go back together."

"What?"

"Everyone is free to leave, or to stay, as long as they wish. We just show you the clubs. It's your choice what to do from there."

I was surprised by their remarks. It wasn't at all what I was expecting.

I went back over to my new friends. "Hey. We can go back anytime," I told the girls.

"The sooner the better," said Rasa.

"Okay, let's leave then."

Rasa and I started for the door, but Jeanie hesitated. "I want to stay. Maybe try to have a good time tonight."

"Really?"

"I'll watch her," Janet interjected quickly. "Don't worry."

"Okay."

"Be safe!" Jeanie called after us, as Rasa and I walked away.

*

"I can find the way back," I announced to Rasa, reaching into my purse and pulling out the map of Miami I had snagged from the hostel check-in.

"We don't need that," countered Rasa, who was purse-and-phone-free. "I remember the way."

"Want to get a cab?"

"No. I love to walk, as you know," she said.

"You sure that's safe?"

"Yes. People are too drunk to touch us," she claimed, striding swiftly and confidently. "You can take cab, if you want."

Rasa had told me that she was also an only child like me, and I could see some of my qualities in her. She did what she pleased, she was independent, and she enjoyed her own company— even while walking alone in a strange country in the dark! I was pretty tired from our Everglades tour, morning walk, and dancing...too tired to protest. So I walked with her back to the hostel.

"Meet you at breakfast?" I asked her.

"Of course. Then we go to the beach, okay?"

"Okay."

*

At around nine a.m. the next morning, I was one of the first in the room to wake up. I still hadn't formally met any of my roommates, but I knew that they existed because I could see their slumbering silhouettes against the already blazing morning sun peeping through the window. I put my bikini on underneath a light summer dress and went down the stairs, excited to have people to eat my chocolate chip pancakes with.

When I got down the stairs, only two of my three new friends were there to greet me. Janet was clutching her cell phone.

"Hey," I said, joining them on the couch by the coffee table with my plate of hot, fresh pancakes. "Where's your sister, Janet?"

"I don't know," she admitted, as she looked over at me with bloodshot eyes.

"What?"

"She went home with someone last night and now she's not answering her phone."

"Did you tell the staff?"

Janet nodded taciturnly. "They said they'd be on it."

Connor came down the stairs and sauntered over to the coffee table.

"Your sister was *crazy* drunk last night!" he said to Janet.

"Do you know where she is?"

Connor shrugged and left.

The Norwegian staff member with the afro came by. "Is your sister back yet? No? ...Okay, this happens sometimes. I'll bang on all the doors. She could be in another room," he said peremptorily. He started off, then turned around and greeted Rasa and me briefly. "Did you like the clubs? No, right? I know—too smelly," he said with a nod, then he hurried off.

"He's cool," I said to Rasa. Then I turned to Janet. "Don't worry, maybe he'll find her."

"I'm a little worried."

"Does she do this type of thing in Belgium?"

Janet nodded.

"Then? She's fine," Rasa declared.

"You're probably right. But...in Belgium, we're home. Here in this strange place...I can't help but worry. Oh, wait a minute! It says here she just signed on Facebook, and she's listening to music. Let me send her a message."

After we finished our pancakes, the staff member returned.

"No luck. I woke up a lot of people, but none of them were Jeanie," he said compassionately.

"Did she ever answer your message?" I asked Janet.

"No. I don't understand. Where is she? She should be back by now."

Rasa collected our finished plates into a neat pile. "Let's just get out of here. Go to the beach. No sense sitting here, waiting, worrying. Who knows? She may be back when *we're* back."

"Okay..." said Janet reluctantly.

"Good. Avoiding the beach in Miami...it is a *sin*!"

*

As soon as we reached the beach, the three of us instinctively took off our flip flops. I was in love with the feeling of the fine grains of sand against my feet.

"Nature's pedicure," joked Janet.

I smiled at her and gave her a comforting rub on the shoulder.

Whether observing fashion, cars, or natural beauty, all the colours in Miami were vivid. That day, like all my days in Miami, there was a clear blue sky that blended almost seamlessly with the offing, contrasting sharply with the white sand of the shore.

We left our towels and dresses by the shore and glided through the shallow water. We kept going until it was chest-high.

I started chatting with Janet about our favourite books to get her mind off her sister. She was fascinated by the Orient. She told me that her favourite author was Khaled Hosseini, a bestselling novelist who wrote about Afghanistan. It struck a chord with her because she used to be a nurse for the Belgian army and had served in Afghanistan.

"We helped everybody. Belgian, Afghani, Canadians like you...We didn't discriminate. Everybody."

"I love Khaled Hosseini too. Did you read *A Thousand Splendid Suns*?"

I didn't mention this to the girls, but the book was actually titled after a line by a well-travelled Persian poet who I was pretty sure had read *The Bhagavad Gita*, 11.12.

"I haven't read Hosseini's new one yet," she confessed. "But I do read a lot of nonfiction about Afghanistan as well, because I love to learn about other cultures. Afghanistan was an amazing country once, with its old Buddha statues and ghazal poetry. Then they utterly trashed the country. I don't know what happened..."

"Do you think it will ever be free again?"

"Of course. That's what we're all hoping and fighting for. And after this, I will get to see another side to Asia. After L.A., we'll start with the Philippines. I can't wait to experience another new culture."

"What about you, Rasa? What books do you like?"

"You know, what's it called? New Age, spiritual, self-help. That sort of thing."

"Oh, cool! You might like *The Bhagavad Gita*."

"I have never heard of this book. Is it Tibetan?"

"Not particularly. It's for everybody. I'll show you my copy later on."

A beach ball splashed beside us.

"Okay. Oh...I think we've caught someone's attention," Rasa noted, grabbing the ball.

A man waded through the water toward us.

"*Ho-la* ladies," he greeted, making the mistake of pronouncing the "h." I wasn't sure where he was from, but he definitely wasn't Latino.

"I saw you way over here, *more-ee-endo* of boredom. You wanna play ball with me?" he asked.

"Oh no." Rasa tossed him his beach ball. "We prefer to just swim."

"You girls are way too dull!" he chirped.

I thought that insults were a strange pick-up tactic. Although, I did admire his guts for approaching three girls without even a wingman.

"Come on," he tried again. "You must like to party. Everybody likes to party."

"We partied more than enough last night," responded Janet dourly.

"Alright. Well, if you ever want to come back to my place, smoke some weed, knock a few back, I could give you my *noo-mero day te-lay-fono*."

"Sorry, we have no notepad. Talk to you later, okay?" Rasa responded, gently but firmly.

The man shrugged and threw his ball at another group of girlfriends before swimming off.

Janet finally allowed herself to laugh.

*

When we swam back to the shore, I saw a figure sitting by our towels and beach bag full of knick knacks. As we neared, I saw it was a petite woman dressed in a baggy tee and oversized sunglasses. Her bleach blonde hair was swept to the side in a messy pony.

"Jeanie?" said Janet, visibly relieved.

"Oh hi," she said casually.

"How was last night?" her sister pressed.

"Fun. Oh—you would not believe what happened in our room just now. The Korean girl had a fight with the crazy Spanish one who went dancing alone."

"She wasn't alone—" I started, but Jeanie cut me off.

"—That Korean is even nuttier than her. She screamed at the Spanish girl until the Spanish girl slapped her. Then the Korean said she would cut herself with a knife from the kitchen..."

As Jeanie continued talking, I could see Janet let it go. What else happened last night with Jeanie was no longer up for discussion. Rasa, Janet and I wrapped ourselves in towels, and the four of us walked back to the hostel together.

*

That evening, my comrades and I sat around the coffee table on our laptops in our loungewear. I had packed the perfect pair of pyjama shorts for Miami: imprinted on them were the phrases "love in the water," and "hope under the sun." Janet said she had packed the same pair, which she had bought in a Belgian outlet mall.

I checked emails, signed in to CouchSurfing.org, and looked into more touristy things to do with the girls in Miami. Tomorrow would be my last day with them. Rasa was boarding a late flight back to Lithuania, and Jeanie and Janet were going to L.A. the next morning.

I received an email update about a position I had applied for almost a month ago in Toronto. I was finally getting a reply after sending a follow up voicemail and a cordial "pleased to meet you" post-interview email. It was another rejection letter, but this time it didn't hurt. It felt like it was a letter sent to another person from another life, for a job that was never meant to be mine. Despite that it was marked "to: me," it felt like the email wasn't addressed to me at all. The rejection had no bearing on me.

What did surprise me were the dozens of new messages I had received from Miami men on my CouchSurfing.org account.

One of the responses was particularly colourful:

Hello Samita, you fireball!

I am a six-figure earner with a gym membership and a great beach body. I'd love to take you to the beach, out to dinner, and out to all the best nightclubs. You can stay at my place as long as your little heart desires.

Awaiting your spicy reply,

Damien

"What the hell is this?" I exclaimed, fighting back a laugh.

"What, what? Show us," Rasa commanded.

I turned my laptop toward the girls.

"*Ugh*...what a liar. No profile pic? If any of this was true, he could say it all with a picture," Janet deduced, rolling her light blue eyes.

"Yes he could, if income and beach body status was even relevant on a website like CouchSurfing!" I added.

"Gonna meet him?" Jeanie probed with a smile.

"Not if you paid me."

"Good!" said Janet, a little forcefully.

Rasa and Jeanie laughed.

*

Connor came down and nodded at all of us.

"Hey ladies...hey drunkie," he said, addressing Jeanie. "You sure had a good time last night."

"I did," Jeanie admitted, with insouciance. "We will go to the beach again tomorrow morning. Want to come?"

I grimaced a little at how hard she was trying.

"No thanks. How's it going, Rasa?"

"Fine. Samita is looking for things we can see tomorrow. Maybe just go to the mall."

Jeanie wasn't about to give up so easily.

"Yes," she said. "I need to buy a new belly ring. I have worn this one for years."

She lifted her shirt to reveal her taut, bejewelled tummy.

"Nice gut. Looks like you had a few too many beers last night," he sneered, having a seat on the couch beside me.

"*So* rude," Janet muttered under her breath, shaking her head.

"*Aaaah!*" he gasped, outstretching his arms as I continued typing up a response email to Keshav, who was curious about how things were in Miami.

Out of the blue, I felt something. I whipped my head to the side, and noticed stubby, reddish fingers on my shoulder.

I got up silently and walked over to the couch beside Rasa.

"Whoa...I freaked that chick out," Connor noted, looking impressed with himself. Then he reclined on the couch and kicked his feet up. "Couch to myself—my plan all along!"

Awkward.

I continued typing in silence, while Rasa made a phone call and Janet shut her laptop, looking irritated. I hoped that Connor would leave soon.

"Hey sexy ladies," said a pretty boy, walking over to us. He took a seat on the couch with Jeanie. "How you feelin', baby?"

"Great."

"I heard you're the type who likes to party. Ever been with a black man before?"

Well, he's direct, I thought to myself.

"No."

"Want to give it a try?"

"No."

"Why not?"

"I prefer blond, blue eyed...I want to find someone who looks like me."

"Then you're missing out on the D."

"Missing what?"

I couldn't believe this conversation was lasting so long. I wondered why Jeanie continued engaging him.

"You know what I'm talking about. It's *this* big," he said, measuring a distance with his hands that was well over a foot.

"Yeah *right!*" I shouted suddenly, before I could stop myself. I cupped a hand to my mouth.

Oops.

"What is it, baby? You don't believe me? I could show you."

I had just inserted myself in the world's most unpleasant conversation. I decided I'd try to shut it down, if possible.

"I'm not interested, sweetheart."

"Why not? You should loosen up, be more like your friend here," he said, brushing his arm against Jeanie.

"Or you could just leave us both alone, please. Learn how to take 'no' for an answer."

"What's the matter, baby face? You never been with a real man before? How old are you, anyway?"

"She said to leave her alone. I suggest you go," interjected a tall, tan man with a Londoner accent. I had run into him a few times and given him perfunctory smiles at breakfast, but we had never spoken. He walked up from behind me to the back of the couch, leaning his hands against the back of it, just over where I was sitting.

"What's it to you?" retorted the pretty boy who knew he was pretty. "I'm just having a little chat with my friends."

"No, she's my friend, and she asked you to leave. I say you should."

I wanted to thank the Englishman for trying, but Pretty Boy wasn't going to back down.

I shut my laptop and stood up. "You know what? It's getting pretty late. I'm just going to call it a night. I'll see you girls at breakfast."

"We didn't make our plan!" Rasa pointed out, standing to follow me.

"It's okay. We'll just go to the beach, and decide what to do from there."

I began walking up the stairs when Rasa caught me by the hand. All three boys were within earshot.

"Samita, is something wrong?"

I laughed and gestured for my runway-tall friend to come close so I could whisper in her ear.

"Nothing's wrong, it's just...there's too much testosterone in this room right now."

She nodded, speaking loudly. "Yes, go to sleep. I think I will do the same."

"We should go, too," said Janet to Jeanie.

Before I continued down the hall, I looked back to find the tall chap, the pretty boy, and the dickhead looking dejected. The Englishman looked like he wanted to ruin Pretty Boy's pretty face.

Way too much testosterone.

Lying with my friends under the scorching morning sun, I looked down at my hands. It appeared that even high-end Dior nail polish couldn't withstand the hours I spent bathing in the salty ocean waters.

Jeanie confessed that she still wasn't feeling well from her wild night.

"There's something therapeutic about the ocean," I observed.

Jeanie and I spent three hours soaking in the ocean water, Rasa and Janet joining us periodically. When Jeanie was ready, we returned to the shore to dry off and go for lunch. My once caramel brown skin had turned an impressive shade of lobster red.

"I hope you ladies have been washing your hair every morning in the shower. The salt is not good for it," Janet lectured.

Rasa and Jeanie nodded, but I looked sheepish.

"...Samita?" Janet beckoned.

"I haven't been shampooing every day. Sometimes I rinse it, though," I confessed.

"Lucky genetics," Janet theorized, running a finger through my damp, dark brown locks. "Where are we going for lunch?"

"Let's have American style. I want hamburger!" announced Rasa.

"Okay," said Jeanie.

Foods dear to those in the mode of goodness increase the duration of life, purify one's existence and give strength, health, happiness and satisfaction. Such foods are juicy, fatty, wholesome, and pleasing to the heart.

Food prepared more than three hours before being eaten, food that is tasteless, decomposed and putrid, and food consisting of remnants and untouchable things is dear to those in the mode of darkness.

—The Bhagavad Gita, 17.8, 17.10

As we started down Ocean Drive, I begged the girls to reconsider. I was a shy person in general, but very outspoken about animal rights issues—namely the cruel, environmentally destructive practice of animal consumption.

"I'm a vegetarian! I can't have a burger with you!" I pleaded.

"You can order something else," Rasa suggested. "I found a busy place with good rating."

I recounted the stench in the air when Drew cooked his burger in the loft that evening. The rancid stench of a *single* burger. I shuddered with disgust at the thought of what the inside of a crowded burger joint would smell like on a day with a high of thirty-five degrees Celsius.

"I...I just can't. Can't we go for pizza?"

"For the Italians. We are in America," said Rasa.

"I'm almost a vegetarian!" proclaimed Jeanie. "I am very into fitness, but...we are on vacation. Why have European food?"

"And you?" I asked Janet.

"I stay with my sister. As much as she lets me," she replied. I noted that she was still miffed from the events of the night before last.

"Okay..." I stopped, standing still on the sidewalk. "Then I'll see you back at the hostel."

Jeanie looked at me apologetically. She gave me a hug.

"Why don't you go and finish planning something for us to do this evening? Anything you want."

"Yeah, I should get back to that. Okay, see you later."

*

I walked back to the hostel and found a fast-food Spanish place nearby. It wasn't everyday that I ate tacos in Canada, so I went inside. I imagined that my European friends had used the same logic when selecting that burger joint.

"Hi. Do you have bean tacos?"

The woman looked at me incredulously. I looked down at the options behind the counter: square metal tubs of meat, meat, meat, lettuce, meat...

"Do you have anything for vegetarians?" I tried once more.

She continued to stare at me. "No English!" she commanded.

I tried to remember the word for "meat," then the words for "vegetarian food," but I was put on the spot.

"Soy...una...vegetariana..." I said slowly.

"Eres vegetariana?" the woman responded, with *fluidez*. "Ohhhh, pero no hay nada. Lo siento."

I left, and found a pizza place. I ordered a cheese slice with no toppings.

"Two dollars!" said the pizza man. He had a Spanish accent, but he could speak a bit of English.

I reached into my purse.

Nada.

I realized I had left all my money locked away in my suitcase.

"Can I use a credit card?" I asked.

The man thought a moment. "No good for business...but I like you. You use."

I smiled. "Gracias."

*

I wanted to do something original and different from the party madness and materialism of Miami. I didn't really want to go to the mall or check out all the shops in Key West. I missed the spiritual atmosphere of the temple.

I typed "Miami temple" into Google.

Just my luck. Not only was there a Miami temple, but they had a program that very evening in honour of the birthday of Lord Balarama, Krishna's elder brother. I noted down the address and asked the spiky haired staff member how to get there. Apparently, it was a somewhat long and complicated journey.

I heard a voice behind me.

"Where are you going?"

I turned around. It was the chap from the night before.

"I'm taking the girls to a temple. Want to come?"

"Hmmm...I've got plans tonight. Maybe we'll hang out another time."

I sat down on the couch, surfing the net while I waited.

"I'm Charlie," said the Englishman, sitting down on the chair next to me. "I'm from Manchester. Where are you from?"

"I'm Samita from Canada."

"A great destination! I'll be stopping there soon enough. I've been travelling for over three years. I just got back from a year in South America."

"What! That's crazy!"

"Want a beer? I could go upstairs and get one."

"No thank you. I don't drink."

"Oh! I'm terribly sorry! I don't drink much either."

"It's fine."

"I wouldn't want you to think I'm one of those crazy drunks. I'm practically a teetotaler. I haven't had anything to smoke in ages, and I rarely drink. I was just offering."

I laughed. He was over apologizing, which was kind of endearing. "Really, it's no big deal. So three years, eh?"

"Samita, you haven't seen anything. In hostels like this, you'll meet people that have been travelling for over a decade."

Charlie went onto his laptop and added me as a friend on CouchSurfing.org and Facebook.

"I've been touring the United States for some time. Miami is a welcome change. Similar vibe to South America, but much more fancy."

"I wouldn't know," I said with a shrug.

"Do you like it here?" he asked, while he shifted around in his seat.

"Not really. Honestly, it feels very fake. I had a hard time making friends and finding things to do when I first arrived."

"I guess people can be a bit rude. Like that arrogant sod from last night."

"Forget him. How's your Spanish, *chico*?"

"It's alright. Hola, hasta luego, cómo estás...that sort of thing. How's yours, *chica*?"

"Not bad. I learned whatever I know *en línea*, so it's far from fluent."

"That's cool. Well, I'll be off. Hope to run into you again!"

I thought Charlie was a fascinating person. I also hoped I would see him again, and that we'd get to hang out more.

Before I went upstairs to shower and change and tell the girls about the plan I'd made for us, I decided to download some new music. Classic rock will always be my road trip music of choice, but it just wasn't suited for Miami. I loaded up my phone with over an hour of reggaeton.

*

New-Age Rasa, free-spirited Jeanie, and the culturally curious Janet were an easy sell on the temple idea.

"Whenever you're ready, we'll go!" said Rasa, who was wearing a nuclear green tank and a cobalt blue skirt.

Jeanie and Janet were still in crocheted beachwear.

"Maybe it's better if you get changed first. It's nice to wear something a little more formal to a temple," I suggested, as politely as I could.

"Formal. No problem!" said Jeanie, taking Janet by the hand.

"I'm fine," said Rasa, unaware that she wasn't the one I was talking about.

The sisters came back five minutes later, dressed for a funeral. It wasn't what I meant by "formal," and I regretted saying anything.

I brushed it off; maybe their Belgian church had an all-black dress code. Besides, we were getting late.

*

Riding the bus to the Metromover, I had a revelation. It was almost the end of the month, and Aunt Flow hadn't come to visit.

"I skipped my time of the month," I whispered to my friends, who smiled and congratulated me.

"Mine is late, too," admitted Janet. "It comes with the nomadic life."

We passed Indian Creek, a lavish area with mansions the size of castles overlooking manicured lawns by a creek where homeowners could park their yachts. I couldn't put my finger on what, but there was something seedy about the area that bubbled just beneath the flashy surface.

"Next time you see me in Miami, you won't find me at hostel. I will travel in style, on a boat like this, with rich husband," Rasa proclaimed.

"Or you could just start a business and make your own money," I said with a smile, jabbing her playfully on the arm. It was an option that I was starting to take more and more seriously.

Rasa ignored me, looking wistful. "Everybody comes to America. Cubans, Mexicans, Chinese, Italians...Why not me? When will I find my dark prince?" she bemoaned.

"Just make sure you really get to know whoever you marry, whether American or Lithuanian."

"Why you say that?"

"Because you never really know what some people will do for money..."

I thought back to Shyam, my first real try at an adult relationship.

Pathetic.

"Money can change people," I asserted.

"You think people commit crimes for this money?" asked Rasa, looking out at the creek.

"All I'm saying is, a house with a boat by a creek, that leads out into the open ocean...it's a better back-door escape plan than most people have."

Rasa laughed. "You have a writer's mind, Samita."

If I ever come across that bus driver again, I will thank her profusely for her wise advice. Making friends with girls and taking them everywhere was the best way to spend my time in Miami. It was nice to be around people that I could talk to so openly. I had had some good conversations with Keshav and Sachin, but I couldn't imagine discussing marriage plans or telling them about my monthly visitor.

*

"Where you girls headed?" asked a friendly older woman with cornrows, entering the Metromover.

I told her about the temple and the subsection where it was located.

"What! Oh, you better be careful. I ain't never heard of a temple, church, or nothing up there. That place is known for nothing but crime."

"What kind of crime?" I asked, although I didn't really want to know.

"Well, I've only been a few times, and I was thrice held at gunpoint."

I saw Jeanie's round eyes widen.

"I beat 'em off. The third time though, they actually robbed me." The woman waved her hand. "You girls will be fine. You can fight, right?"

Jeanie and I gaped at her nervously.

"I can!" declared Rasa.

"Just stick together. No one will mess with you. And if you can, have someone walk you back."

"What kind of temple is this?" Janet asked me, after the woman arrived at her stop.

"Hare Krishna."

"Hare Krishna!" gasped Rasa.

"You've heard of us?"

"Oh yes of course! Everyone in Lithuania knows. And I don't much care for it. So pushy and noisy, singing and dancing on the street like crazy people...Do you do that, too? That parade thing?"

"Yep. I'm one of the crazy street dancers," I said unabashedly. "Not pushy, though."

"You're a *little* pushy," countered Rasa. "When it comes to your vegetable diet."

"Okay, fair enough," I admitted. "Just wait a few years; as the world becomes more advanced, there will be more people like me."

Jeanie shrugged. "That's probably true. I could easily be a vegetarian."

Although Rasa already found me pushy, upon my return, my commitment to my vegetarian diet and animal rights advocacy was only fortified when I started my writing business. Entrepreneurship helped me grow my confidence and develop the gumption to use my voice and my skills to stand up for animals. Had I gotten my dream post-graduation job as an editorial assistant for a Big Five publisher, this would never have happened for me. I would have allowed myself to get too "comfortable." I could feel it happening, and Krishna wouldn't allow it to happen. I had to grow both as a person finding her voice and as a professional making her mark in the world.

*

The temple was located in a residential neighbourhood, a good walk away from where the Metromover stopped. I made a mental note to find someone to walk us back. Rasa may not have minded, but after the woman's warning, I did not want to walk back alone in the dark.

If the neighbourhood was supposed to be a ghetto, it certainly didn't look like one. We passed beautiful, colorful, two-storey suburban homes as we walked down the sidewalk, looking for the correct house number. When we were a few houses away, we heard the *kirtan*—devotional singing in praise of Lord Krishna. When we entered the temple and took off our shoes, I rushed to the deities of The Devine Couple—Lord Krishna and his eternal consort Radha. I bowed before the Lord and began to dance and sing, leaving my friends behind.

Hare Krishna, Hare Krishna,

Krishna Krishna, Hare Hare,

Hare Rama, Hare Rama,

Rama Rama, Hare Hare.

Jeanie ran up beside me and started to dance with me, while Janet and Rasa looked on from the sidelines.

A Spanish girl wearing a sari passed the four of us some pamphlets about karma and vegetarianism. After the *kirtan*, we sat down to watch the bathing of the deity of Lord Balarama.

"Wow," said Janet, reading through one of the flyers. "You never told us that *this* was the reason you didn't want to eat that burger!"

"I think I want to become a vegetarian now. I didn't know that eating meat was so bad for my karma," said Jeanie, alarmed.

Rasa rolled her eyes.

"I should stop drinking too. I don't like the person I become when I drink," Jeanie continued.

We sat on the floor and watched as the golden deity of Lord Balarama was bathed in yogurt, milk, and honey as people sang, clapped their hands, and played musical instruments. Rose petals were then showered over the Lord before He was rinsed with water, covered by a cloth, dressed, and taken away.

*

The four of us sat in the temple's dining area, where a vegetarian feast was served. For dessert, we each took a small cup of the blessed honey and yogurt mixture known as *caranamrita*.

"Oh...this is delicious! At least now I get good meal before my flight," said Rasa.

One of the temple staff approached us with some spiritual books. He made a hard sell for *The Bhagavad Gita*, but Jeanie and

Janet said that they didn't have the room in their luggage. Rasa said that she would read the book online.

"I like these types of books. I am curious, but do not want to buy book at this time. I will read on internet," she told him.

He turned to me. "And you, pretty girl?" He then addressed the others. "What a beautiful friend you have here!"

My three friends nodded enthusiastically. If I wasn't already a decent shade of fire-engine red, I would have blushed. I cleared my throat.

"My copy is right here in my purse."

"In that case, would I be able to interest you in a canto of *The Srimad Bhagavatam*?

My friends looked hesitant.

"I'll take it," I announced. I reached into my purse, and all I had was a five. My preoccupation with not carrying cash for safety reasons had hindered me from donating to a cause I really believed in and supported.

"It's okay," he said, giving me the book.

He was gracious, but I still felt bad because I wanted to make a donation to the temple, and I was pretty sure that I hadn't even covered the printing costs of the book he gave me. I told myself that I would return to this temple again before leaving Miami, and would make a more generous donation.

I wanted to use whatever limited funds I had to help establishments that were trying to serve Lord Krishna, especially after He had done so much for me, guiding me through this beautiful physical and spiritual journey.

Krishna is also known as "Govinda," which means "he who gives pleasure to the cows." This is because approximately five thousand years ago, when Krishna walked the Earth, he was a cowherd boy. His eternal consort Radha was a milkmaid. According to the Vedic tradition, which has roots in ancient India, there are actually seven mothers: our birth mother, our guru's wife, the wife of any priest, any nurse, the queen, Mother Earth, and Mother Cow, who gives us milk. Cows are honoured and protected by followers of Lord Krishna, who use cow milk in divine rituals such as deity bathing. As a follower of Lord Krishna, I could not tolerate animal cruelty, or patron a burger joint, where I knew the owners were profiting against something I was fundamentally against.

But Krishna is much kinder and more forgiving than I am, and he brought my friends into his temple home and allowed them to partake of a divine ritual and eat a sumptuous feast even after eating the flesh of his treasured cow friends only hours before.

Lord Krishna, who sees the soul in all people, animals, and other living entities, always amazed me with his kindness.

The humble sages, by virtue of true knowledge, see with equal vision a learned and gentle brāhmaṇa, a cow, an elephant, a dog and a dog-eater [outcaste].

—The Bhagavad Gita, 5.18

Three young, Latino men clad in traditional Indian *dhotis* approached us and pulled up chairs beside us. They were well built, and seemed to be in their late-twenties to early-thirties.

"My name is Alan. These are my friends Alejandro and Jose."

Alejandro nodded a tacit greeting while Jose chatted up Janet. Alan turned his attention to Rasa and me.

"I came here on a boat," he told us.

149

I was taken aback by his unconventional introduction.

"A ship?" I questioned.

"A boat I made myself, with the help of Alejandro here and two other kids. I was eleven. Alejandro was just ten. We left Havana and three days later, here we were in the Land of Milk and Honey." He laughed and raised his sweet drink as if to make a toast. "Now we're permanent residents in a great country, where we are entitled to life, liberty, and the pursuit of happiness."

"That must have been scary...being on that boat," I commented.

He shook his angular head. "The *storms* were scary. There was a storm every night. One night, the ocean took the life of my friend."

"I'm sorry."

Alan shook his head again. "It was Krishna's will," he said disaffectedly. "I came here and joined a Cuban gang. Then I wanted to better myself, and I found God."

"They just let you go like that?"

"Leaving the gang was the easy part. The hardest thing was giving up all the women. Finding God meant losing the women. Most men cannot resist the allure of a beautiful woman."

It seemed that of the challenges in Alan's life, overcoming desire ranked higher than a terror-filled boat ride.

As a strong wind sweeps away a boat on the water, even one of the roaming senses on which the mind focuses can carry away a man's intelligence.

—The Bhagavad Gita, 2.67

*

150

"Are you also from Cuba?" I asked Jose, changing the subject.

"No, I'm from El Salvador."

The temple was starting to close down, so Alan and Jose walked us out. Alejandro drove home. Alan lived in the temple, and Jose lived in South Beach.

"I'll walk you to the bus stop, and Jose will be with you from there," said Alan.

As we walked, he recounted the story of a Hare Krishna monk who had taken over fifty disciples, Alan included, to New Orleans around the time of Mardi Gras.

"Only forty came back. Fifteen were taken in by the beautiful women. Not me though. I know that Krishna will send me a wife. Perhaps a Canadian one."

He gave me a wink, which I pretended not to see in the dark night.

"I have been married before. A Portuguese girl married me for citizenship. In exchange, she was to give me children. But once she got the green card, she was off."

"You didn't marry for love?" Jeanie pried, sounding genuinely shocked. The rest of the hostel had pegged her as a wild woman, but she was such a traditional romantic at heart.

"No. I married her to help her out."

"But you lied. Isn't that bad for your karma?" Jeanie persisted. Apparently, she had taken the pamphlets very seriously.

"It's *good* for my karma; I helped someone. And in time, I'll marry again. My guru says I'm not ready, but I think I am."

"I also feel ready to marry," announced Rasa.

Uh oh.

We arrived at the Metromover. Alan took down my number and Rasa's email before he headed back to the temple. Once we got off at our platform, we walked to the bus stop and waited for the bus to South Beach.

At night, the bus stop was positively terrifying. Homeless people walked around us, encircling us. As the bus took longer and longer, the men started circling closer and closer. I was so glad that I had made friends with girls and taken them everywhere. Going to the temple alone could have ended horrifically.

The men were almost beside us now.

Headlights flashed before us, and a vehicle came to a screeching halt.

The bus had arrived, just in time.

We hopped on, and the homeless men stood and watched us depart. Whatever they were doing, they weren't waiting for the bus.

*

The bus was full of people who had been drinking. Jose took a seat beside a dizzy looking young man with a face tattoo and only one shoe.

"Yo bro, have you seen my shoe?" he asked Jose.

"Nah man. Sorry."

The girls and I sat at the back of the bus, where I could observe rather than be observed.

Rasa was twiddling Alan's contact information in her hands.

"Be careful," I warned. "I think that Alan is pretty messed up."

"Wouldn't you be messed up if you had that life?" asked Jeanie.

I shrugged my shoulders. Maybe I was being harsh. Still, with my intention to return to the temple in the future, I had to stay cautious. As Krishna says, there are a variety of reasons why people turn to God.

O best among the Bhāratas, four kinds of pious men begin to render devotional service unto Me—the distressed, the desirer of wealth, the inquisitive, and he who is searching for knowledge of the Absolute.

—The Bhagavad Gita, 7.16

As we continued on our bumpy bus ride, the jostling made some of the passengers start to retch. Through the sharp turns and ups and downs, I noticed a lone shoe slide into the aisle.

I handed it to the young man.

"Whoa—thanks!" he exclaimed, giving me the thumbs-up. He held his thumb up long after I had returned to my seat.

"She found my shoe!" he told Jose excitedly.

Jose nodded politely.

When we got off the bus, we bade goodbye to Jose and went our separate ways.

"Jose is pretty cute," Jeanie observed.

Rasa concurred.

"I don't know guys. I think *Alejandro* was kind of cute."

My journey was changing me. I found myself opening up to the idea of romance. I had had some raunchy encounters in high school and in my university dorm room, but I had spent the last twenty-three years largely ignoring that part of my life. A dramatic faux-relationship with the high school pot dealer, late-night romps in a campus dorm room, and my fizzled-out fling with Shyam weren't even worth mentioning as true romances. They were temporary unities with low stakes and low commitment.

Now, I wanted passion. True love. And I was ready to get serious about it.

"Who?" asked Rasa.

"Oh, you don't remember?"

"The quiet one?"

"I guess I'm into the strong, silent type."

We said our goodbyes to Rasa in the hallway. Soon, she'd be on board to Lithuania.

"Thank you for taking us out to the temple, Samita," said Janet. "That's the great thing about the hostel. You meet people and do interesting things that aren't included in the tourist pamphlet."

"No—thank *you* girls. This was honestly one of the best days of my life."

Rasa nodded. "It was fun, I guess."

I gave her a hug goodbye, and never saw her again.

*

The next morning, there were only three of us. I ate breakfast with the sisters before we went to the beach together one last time.

"Hey ladies! Want to smoke some weed?" a man called to us as we sunbathed.

"No, gracias," I said.

He laughed. "*No soy Cubano,* honey. I'm Italian. I overstayed my visa. Been here three years now and I run a successful business. Nobody checks when you have money! So what do you say? Are we going to party or what?"

None of us said anything, and the man scowled and walked off.

"That's one thing I won't miss. The ocean, on the other hand...I'll miss that," Janet remarked.

"You can see the ocean in Asia," I said with a smile.

"From the Philippines, we'll see the Pacific. Maybe we'll make a stop in India and see the Indian Ocean, or go to Burma or Thailand. Hopefully the men will be less bothersome."

"I don't mind the attention," confessed Jeanie. "As a whole, women have it better than men. Yes, we're treated like garbage, but we can work it in our favour. Men are suckers. We can dress nicely, get some free stuff..."

"I had no idea you were so jaded," I remarked.

We walked back to the lobby, where I waited with the girls while they packed their things and called a cab. I gave them both a hug goodbye, and wished them luck in L.A. and Asia.

By Myself but Not Alone

I sat down on the couch, on my own once more. I noticed the turnover in my hostel roommates—a group of German girls had just moved in—and my own time in Miami was also coming to an end in the next three days.

I decided not to go anywhere else during my final days. Not Louisiana. Not Texas. Not even some fancy mainland hotel. I just wanted to stay in the hostel, continue exploring Miami, swimming in the ocean, and introspecting.

I went up to the counter to book my bunk bed for three more nights. The spiky haired Norwegian was bent over, talking on his cell phone.

"No, she is not going to be okay...and neither am I. I know, I know...I'm sorry, but I have to go."

He sniveled and wiped his eyes.

"Yes?"

"I'd like to book my room for three more nights, please."

"Of course," he said.

His face was puffy. I pretended not to notice.

To this day I regret not reaching out to him. I didn't want to be nosy, or to push him to talk about something that was obviously painful for him. But did I make the right decision?

Sometimes, it's acknowledging the issues of strangers that reminds us that we're all human.

A dark haired woman in her early twenties was sitting on the couch with her laptop. She beckoned me to come join her.

"Hey. What's up?"

"I'm watching a Bollywood movie. You're Indian, right? Want to watch it with me?"

"Honestly, I don't really like that stuff."

"Why not? It's your culture! I'm from Iran, but I can't get enough of your movies. Indian movies are the best."

"Well, I don't like to watch movies in general. I don't really see watching movies as an important part of preserving my culture. To me, Indian culture is about spirituality."

The Irani girl staunchly disagreed. She had been living at the hostel for a month, and would remain there for some time while she completed an internship. She told me that every night when she came home from work, she loved to sit on the couch and watch film after film, until she eventually fell asleep with her earbuds still in.

"There's no better way to spend an evening," she asserted.

I shrugged. "Sounds boring to me."

Watching movies and TV was an addictive hobby I'd developed before, and I was trying to avoid it because it was a killer of productivity, or even ambition. I didn't want to end up living my life on the sidelines, while all the interesting things happened to my favourite characters on the screen.

The people who know me best say that they doubt I would even pursue writing creatively if I had worked in an office— possibly living my whole life without even completing a single book, being too tired after long days to do much more than eat popcorn and watch sitcoms, the storylines written by wordsmiths who were actually living their dreams.

*

I went upstairs and retrieved my cash from my locked suitcase, which I had yet to remove from the top bunk since I moved in. In fact, I had been sleeping with my suitcase at my feet, my backpack on top of the suitcase, and my purse under my pillow. The only things that I had left out in the open were my toiletries by the shared sink. (Latoya's fear-mongering had gotten to me just a little.)

A couple of my new roommates were inside the room, changing into their bikinis and putting on sunscreen before heading back out. They were speaking to each other in German.

"Hey, do either of you know how to get to the mall?" I asked.

One of the girls stared at me a moment, caught off guard. She couldn't have been over nineteen.

"Mall? Uhh...*yes*," she said. I could see that she was unused to speaking English.

"Okay. How do I go there?"

"Uhh...by bus."

"Okay. Which bus?"

She held up her fingers.

I grabbed my purse, put my cash inside, and ran out the door.

"*Danke!*" I said before it shut.

I took the bus to the Aventura Mall, passing more of Miami's lush sceneries, swanky hotels with fountains out front, and both upscale and middle-class housing. I people-watched the other patrons in the seats around me as I listened to Daddy Yankee on my cell phone. An old man sitting across from me on the bus wore overalls with no t-shirt, a straw hat, and carried a fishing pole and a wicker basket. He gave me a smile.

I strolled through the mall casually. What was the rush? As long as I was back before people started drinking (five or six p.m.), I thought I would be relatively safe as a woman travelling alone. I had a regained sense of confidence, and I was starting to feel comfortable in the City of Miami, with or without girlfriends to take everywhere.

At Aventura, I tried to look for a Wal-Mart so I could have my glasses fixed, but I soon found out that it wasn't that kind of mall. I threw a Canadian penny into the fountain and made a wish that no matter what happened to me in my life, I would never forget Radha and Krishna.

I visited stores that I had only read about in American magazines as a teenager, places like Wet Seal, where I splurged on a colourful pair of jeans.

Should I buy them? I debated with myself. *Why not? I haven't done laundry since Savannah. I could use a cute new pair of jeans.* (I would regret this decision six months later in Canada, when I came across the same pair in the clearance section at Urban Planet.)

I visited an old favourite, Forever XXI. Since I had already almost maxed out my budget for the day, I stuck to the accessory section, where I looked for a small souvenir. Necklaces and bottles of nail polish were being sold for a pittance.

I saw a chain with two pendants: a tiny buffalo skull and what may very well be America's most distinguishable state. The word "Texas" was engraved on the back of the pendant.

I considered buying it. It was cute, and it was inexpensive, and I would surely have worn it—but an inner voice halted me.

You haven't been to Texas—not yet. Save it for when you do go there.

Just in front of the cash register, there was a bin full of nail polish bottles. I picked out a bottle of iridescent sparkles.

"Oh, my favourite!" the cashier commented, showing me her luminous, self-applied manicure. It looked great.

"Wow. How many coats did that take?"

"Just two! Isn't it nice? Something different."

I bought the bottle right away. High-end Dior certainly worked in New York, but there was nothing better suited to Miami than attention-grabbing, shimmery, sparkly glitter.

*

I still had some free time, so I asked a lady at the bus station if she knew how to get to Wal-Mart. She went off at me in quick, fluent Spanish. She pointed to her ears, then she pointed to the ground. I had absolutely no idea what she was saying.

"Sorry, no Spanish," I said.

"Your parents should teach!"

I looked at her, nonplussed.

"*Ah!*" she exclaimed, waving me away.

I asked a bus driver who was standing casually beside the bus he had been driving, taking a break. He told me to hop in, and he'd let me know where to get off once we reached Wal-Mart.

"Do you fix glasses?" I asked, once I reached Wal-Mart's optic center.

"Yes. It will be a hundred and nine dollars."

"That's fine. When can I pick them up?"

"Nine days."

I regretted not making Wal-Mart my first destination when I stepped off the bus from Georgia, ages before.

The Beachside Blow Up

The next morning, there was a huge blow up.

A tall, buff black man entered the hostel with a duffle bag, looking to check in.

Wish Rasa was here, I thought.

The Norwegians weren't working that morning. Another staff member checked his ID, and turned him away.

"Sorry, man. We don't house locals."

The man shouted expletives and racially denigrating remarks, and headed upstairs.

"Hey man! You gotta go!"

The man turned around angrily, glaring at the staff member, who glared right back.

He shouted a final four-letter curse, and opened the door so hard on the way out I thought it would shatter.

A few moments later, a gorgeous woman with long brown hair and soft features walked in. When she checked in, I noticed that she had an English accent, despite that she was about as tan as I was.

"Credit or cash?" the staff member asked her.

"Whichever is easier for you."

"You're pretty nice for a girl."

She laughed nervously.

"Most girls don't like to make things easy for us dudes."

Later on when breakfast started, I saw Charlie. I pulled up a seat beside him.

"What do you have planned for the day?" I asked.

"Not too much. Just going to the beach, then out with the boys," he responded, while he wolfed down his chocolate chip pancakes.

"I was thinking to head to the Vizcaya museum."

"Oh. I'm not much of a museum person. But you can come pubbing with us, if you want."

"I'm not much of a pubbing person."

"Oh. Well, I'm off to the beach. See you around!"

"Wait!"

He turned. "Yes?"

"I'm coming with you! Just let me get my towel and some munchies."

I went back up to my room, grabbed my new nail polish, and pulled out a bag of chips from my locked suitcase. It was against hostel rules to hoard food upstairs, but I had learned the hard way not to leave it in the kitchen. I had brought back blessed temple food so that I could have a nice lunch the next day after the girls left, but that meal was enjoyed by someone else Krishna wanted to bestow his mercy upon.

I hurried back down the stairs. I knew that my wandering, fidgety friend wouldn't wait long for me.

*

"Did something happen in the hostel this morning?" Charlie asked me, as we walked over to the beach together.

"Yeah. This guy tried to check in and the staff turned him away, so he made a bunch of racist comments and stormed out."

"A white guy?"

"No. A black guy."

"He made racist comments to another black guy?"

"No. The staff was white. I think. It's hard to tell."

"Hmm. That was pretty rude of him."

"I guess."

"Was he as arrogant as that sod from the other night?"

"Charlie, I think it's time to forget about that jerk from that night."

We lay on the beach together, sharing an open bag of chips. It was a windy day, and once in a while when I took a bite I could taste the gritty sand that had blown into the bag.

"What's your sign?" asked Charlie.

"I'm a Capricorn."

"I'm a Leo. Do you have a boyfriend?"

"No. Do you?"

He laughed. "No. What do you look for in a man?"

"Maturity. Someone decisive, but also laid-back."

"That sounds like me."

"He also has to be a vegetarian and believe in God."

"I don't follow a specific religion. To me, it's just about being a good person."

Charlie looked at me with a peculiar smile. "You're pretty religious, aren't you?"

"I prefer the term 'spiritual.'"

"So you're one of those born-again Christian types? A good girl?"

I laughed. "Charlie, you clearly do not know me. I'm a pretty wild girl."

"Oh really? So what's the wildest thing you've ever done, crazy girl?"

I thought for a moment.

"I pet a crocodile in northern Ghana."

"Hmm. Yeah that's pretty adventurous."

"And you?"

"I ate crocodile meat when I was in Australia."

"Oh Charlie...that's disgusting."

"Yeah. It wasn't very good," he replied, looking aloof. "You've done a lot for your years, haven't you? How old are you?"

"Twenty-three."

Charlie guffawed. "You're a baby!"

He ceased flirting immediately.

*

"Fancy a swim?" Charlie proposed, throwing off his shirt. He had a tan, undernourished body. The body of a vagabond.

"Wow—you're so dark," I remarked.

"Look at this," he said, pulling down his shorts to reveal a striking tan line that went from a deep, orange-brown to almost paper white.

I gasped. "Gross!" I said, throwing off my own sundress carelessly.

I didn't get the same strange vibes around Charlie that I had with Drew. I appreciated how protective he was when he saw how Pretty Boy was talking to me. I thought of him as a caring, platonic friend.

"Watch out, shark attack!" shrieked Charlie, splashing me with water.

He was also thirty going on thirteen.

Charlie told me that he had funded his two years of travelling with his entrepreneurial efforts. He was also quite frugal, and did a fair amount of couch surfing. He confided in me that he thought his travels were coming to an end. He had seen most of South America, and after seeing the northern part of the Americas, namely the U.S. and Canada, he wanted to go back to England.

Even as he was telling me this, I knew he would never truly return home. There was something restive and shifty about my peripatetic friend. Although he might return to England for some time, sleeping in at his parents' place, getting paler, fatter, and healthier, it wouldn't be long before his foot would start to itch and he'd look out to the sea once more. Wherever he went, he would never be able to lay down roots.

*

166

When we walked back to the shore, an old man called us toward him.

"Look at this! I found a sand dollar!" he said, showing us the beautiful animal, still alive.

"Put that back!" I commanded.

"No way, babe. We never see these things around here anymore."

"That's the point. Let me see that," I said, grabbing it from him before he could protest.

I raised my arm to hurl it back into the ocean, but he snatched it back from me before I could. He gave me a harsh look, and walked off, taking the live sand dollar with him so its skeleton could someday collect dust on one of his shelves. Because of people like him, these remnants will probably someday be all that remain of the species.

"I tried," I said to Charlie, who looked at me with sympathy. I knew he didn't care about animal rights—he preferred to eat crocodiles while I preferred to pet them—but he had my back regardless.

Charlie and I sat in silence as we dried off on the beach. I hunched over with my nail polish bottle, noticing that some fuzzy peach leg hairs were starting to return. I painted my toes with my glistening new polish, perfect for sunny South Beach. I would have done my fingernails as well, but they still had some blue on them.

Nearby, a pretty young woman was reading a book with a German title. A man walked up to her, and started calling her the way that you might call a cat or another domesticated animal. I told myself that if he tried to touch her, I'd say something, but for the time being I kept quiet. Charlie was also silent. The German girl looked at the man, got up, and walked away. I regretted not being more vocal.

A few minutes later she returned.

"Hey, sorry about that guy!" I yelled to her.

"It's okay," she said calmly. "He followed me. He wanted me to give him five dollars. I said 'no' and he left."

"What?" said Charlie, bemused.

"Probably a bogus 'club entrance' fee," I reasoned, popping a sandy chip into my mouth.

I lay back on the towel, soaking up the sun and sand. I was about to put my hat over my face, when I saw the hostel staff from that morning out of the corner of my eye. He was walking toward us.

"Hey guys. Mind if I sit with you?"

I sighed.

He took a chip. "I'm on break. I just can't sit on the beach by myself, you know? I'd die of boredom."

"I could do it all day," I said.

"Must be a chick thing."

"Are you the bloke who had to deal with that episode this morning?" Charlie asked him.

"Yeah. Some people are just too ridiculous. It's people like that who are the reason I started doing MMA."

"I don't think I've seen you around the hostel before. Where are you from?" I asked him.

"Montreal. Girls are really nice up there. Not like here, with these European French bitches. You're in the room with the Germans, right?"

"Yes," I answered.

I looked around. Thankfully, the German girl from before was gone. I could already sense his reaction.

"Real stuck up bitches, those German girls."

I tossed my dress over my head and put on my flip flops. My hair was still wet, so I wrapped it up in a makeshift turban with my towel.

"I should go. See you later, Charlie."

"Wait, do you want your chips?" asked the staff, handing me the almost-empty bag.

"You keep it."

*

I took the scenic Metromover to the Vizcaya museum, which used to be the estate of a prominent businessman in the early nineteen hundreds. He died shortly after its completion. It went on to become a large museum and garden area that looked more like an Italian castle than a home. I didn't much like the inside of the house/castle; it was old, dark, and kind of eerie, furnished with dreary old-fashioned knick-knacks.

Who lives like this? I wondered.

I preferred the outside, where I sat down in Vizcaya's idyllic gardens, overlooking the vast ocean, and wrote in my journal.

I hadn't seen the ocean too many times in my life, but in Miami I was seeing it every day. Still, it never ceased to amaze me.

It's interesting how as we travel, new people come into our lives who can be such a major character for one day, or two, or thirty, before they leave our life story, sometimes never to return. Now that the digital age has made the world considerably smaller, a few characters might make another appearance in a supporting role, while most are gone forever. For a few days on my journey, I was thick as thieves with three girlfriends, and I valued the time I spent with them. But now, I was back to being a solo traveler. As we move from place to place in this life, meeting new people and leaving old ones behind, in the grander scheme of things our souls move from body to body, losing old connections and making new ones.

As a person puts on new garments, giving up old ones, the soul similarly accepts new material bodies, giving up the old and useless ones.

—The Bhagavad Gita, 2.22

Unconventional Protection

I woke up the next morning and ate my pancakes out on the patio rather than on the couch. I sat at the table under the umbrella with my breakfast, my purse, and my *Gita*.

Even if I couldn't find much else to do during my final full day in Miami, as long as I made it to the temple, that was all that mattered to me. It was my one final goal before I could call my trip complete.

It was early and not too many other people were awake, but there was another woman on the patio with me, sweeping the floor in exchange for free nights at the hostel. She was a nomadic vision, with sun-parched skin, bleach-blonde hair with a light streak of pink on one side, and a white peasant top and cut-off jean shorts. She was also the only forty-something woman I've ever seen that could pull off that tweenish glitter eye-shadow with ease and confidence. I chatted with her for a bit about things to do in town, and she suggested the Vizcaya museum.

"Thanks," I said politely.

Scrolling through my emails, I noticed a new message from an employment agency I had registered with. They wanted to know if I was available for a job interview sometime next week.

I hit the "delete" button and checked out what was new on Facebook. I was friends with the trio I had met at the temple, and going through Alan's profile, I noticed that ninety percent of his other friends were underage girls with beachside profile pics.

I heard footsteps coming toward me.

"Hey baby face."

I didn't need to look up. I already knew that it was none other than Pretty Boy.

"It's *this* big," he said to me, likely gesturing with his hands. I kept my eyes on my *Gita*, but I knew that there was no way he would have taken the hint.

He took a seat beside me. "What you readin', baby?"

"Nothing," I said, shutting the book.

This was the only time in my life that I *didn't* want to show someone *The Bhagavad Gita*.

"You know what? You're pretty rude," he said.

I opened my book again. "Thanks hun."

He got up and walked off in a huff, never bothering me again.

*

I went up to my room to wash my hair. Miami was so hot that even when set to cold, the shower water ran warm. When I stepped out, a girl at the shared sink asked me if I had any toothpaste.

"This is my bag," I told her, opening the pink, zippered bag for travel cosmetics. "Any time you need toothpaste, you can take it from here."

"Thank you!"

I heard my phone buzz, and I fished it of my purse by my pillow. I had a text message from Alan:

"Samita...r u coming to the temple tonight 4 d Sunday program?"

I texted back, "I'll see."

I rushed over to Charlie's room and knocked on the door.

"Oh hi, Samita!" He greeted me cheerily. "Want to grab a bite?"

"Charlie, I want to go to the temple tonight. Will you come with me?"

"I don't know..."

"Please? It's quite a ways by bus and I don't really feel safe going by myself."

Charlie looked at me with concern. "Okay. Just come knock on the door when you're ready to go."

I went back to my bunk. Sitting over the edge with my legs dangling, I thought hard. I knew that when I knocked on Charlie's door later that night, he wouldn't be there. As much as he cared about me, he had no control over his itchy, itinerant feet. I would be surprised if I found him in his room even ten minutes later.

I texted Alan.

"What time should I come? ...Don't want to take the bus late."

"Alejandro will pick u & Jose up."

I went down to the lobby. It was time to get social.

It was about noon, but many people were already sitting around sipping on bottles of beer. I looked around for a friendly face.

"Krishna?" asked a young Asian man. He had recognized the background pic I had on the cell phone I was clutching.

Yes! Maybe this was my chance.

"Are you interested in spirituality?"

"Yes. I Buddhism," he said.

"Do you want to come with me to the temple tonight?"

"I leave soon for China. I wait taxi."

I sighed.

It was too late to make friends. The girls were gone, and if I still wanted to go to the temple, I had a choice to make:

I could either, a) get into a car with men I didn't know very well, with at least one them being a former gang member, or b) I could get into a bus with people I have never met before, with likely more than one being a *current* gang member.

I got out my phone to text Alan.

"How early can you pick me up?" I wrote.

*

It was about three in the afternoon, and Alan would be coming shortly. He told me that it was okay to be at the temple early if we all agreed to help out with some temple service: cleaning the floors, wiping the tables, that sort of thing. I liked to travel in daylight, so I happily agreed. In any case, I wanted to do something nice for the temple. I also made sure that I brought a decent amount of cash with me this time so that I could make a better donation.

I certainly didn't want to go to the temple empty handed, in more ways than one.

The feeling that there was something off about Alan was unshakable, and he was clearly the leader among his friends. I didn't trust him farther than I could've thrown him. And unlike Rasa, I wasn't born without the fear factor.

I received another text: "Jose is w8ing 4 u outside."

I searched my suitcase for my little bottle of makeshift mace. It had spilled and dried, leaving a light, spicy scent in the inside compartment. I needed a backup plan.

"Auf wiedersehen!" I said to my roommate, before rushing out the door and down the steps to the kitchen.

I looked around; there were endless numbers of knives, but how quickly could a knife get turned on me if I was in a car with three fairly well-built men?

And then I saw it: a large, spray bottle of soap by the sink. It was unexpected. It would throw any attacker off guard. It would impair their vision long enough to kick them where it hurt.

I shoved the bottle into my purse, barely managed to zip it shut, and went out the door to meet Jose. Within a few moments, Alejandro and Alan arrived to pick us up in a red hatchback.

*

Jose was acting giggly, and his breath smelled; he had obviously been drinking. I started to feel uneasy.

Who drinks before going to a temple?

...Or did the boys have something else in mind for the evening?

We drove across the bridge to mainland Miami, with the awesome ocean beneath us and the high rise buildings in front of us. We passed familiar locales, and within ten minutes, we were at the temple. I breathed a sigh of relief.

An orange-clad *sannyasi* (monk) looked me up and down. The orange garments indicated a vow of celibacy, while white garments were for the *grihasthas* (householders). I looked down at my own clothes self-consciously: a flowery belly top and artfully

175

ripped, bright yellow capris. It was one of my last remaining clean outfits.

"Sí?" he asked.

"My friend here is visiting from Canada," said Alan. "She wants to help."

He continued to stare at me blankly.

"Sí. Quiero...ayudarle," I said, in broken, accented Spanish.

The sannyasi smirked. He got up, and tossed me a dry rag. He started speaking fluent Spanish with Alan.

"He wants you to clean tables," Alan told me.

Alan and his best friends went to get changed into their *dhotis*, making me look even more out of place in my beachy gear. Alan took my purse and said he'd keep it safe in the men's *ashram*.

"Whoa, heavy purse!" he remarked, as he took it from my hand. "What's in here, anyway?"

"This and that," I responded nonchalantly.

We went to complete our respective chores. I got to work on the tables, but since the rag was dry, it was more like dusting than washing. When we all went to report back to the sannyasi, he looked less than impressed.

"He said you didn't clean it properly," Alan revealed to me.

"Not my fault!" I protested.

Alan paused. "You're right," he decided. "He should've given you some water, or told you where to get some."

I approached the sannyasi.

"Otra oportunidad?" I asked.

He pursed his lips. "No. That's enough for today. You guys relax, get something to eat, and come back for the kirtan," he said fluently.

I looked at him, stunned.

"I have other people to help," he revealed, as if trying to contain a laugh. "I wanted to give you a chance. You know, since you asked so nicely, *in Spanish*."

I stood there awkwardly, not knowing how to respond.

"Come, Samita," said Alan, giving me a slap on the shoulder. "Let's go to Taco Bell."

"Alright, just get me my purse."

*

Alejandro drove us to a nearby Taco Bell to get some burritos. I began to unzip my purse to pay, but Alan waved me off.

"Alejandro will pay," he told me.

I let my crush pick up the tab for the one-dollar meal.

We said a prayer before we ate. Jose laughed, questioning whether or not I could pronounce the Sanskrit words.

"Leave her alone," said Alan.

We started to eat.

"Ew...onions!" I squealed, picking them out of the burrito.

Jose laughed. "She doesn't like onions!"

I wasn't sure what was so funny.

Jose and Alan were full of things to say to me, but Alejandro was the one I was really curious about. I wondered how I could start up a conversation with him.

After lunch, we walked around the temple grounds, which were filled with beautiful flowers. Alan introduced me to the temple cat, and when I told him I was a cat person, he let me pet her. I noticed that she was suffering from worms.

"Only the cats are allowed to be non-vegetarian, not people," he commented.

I nodded in agreement.

"I used to bring in lots of these stray cats. The temple didn't mind. Then I started bringing in stray humans, and I got some push-back."

"Stray humans?"

"Yes. Former gangsters like myself. The homeless. People who wanted to turn their life around. People that I felt had potential. People who were lost, like I was."

"What did you say to them?"

"I asked them if they wanted to come and stay with me, in a nice place, get a good meal...Most people didn't want to. They see a meatless meal and they say 'no way.' But I helped those who wanted to be helped."

"Why did the temple make you stop?"

"Some had mental issues. They were causing too many problems."

I shrugged. "I guess you would have to be pretty crazy to turn down delicious temple food."

I knew that Alan was looking for a wife, and my guard was *way* up. I also questioned how genuine he was. I resolved to remain cordial, but distant with him.

Maybe Alan truly wanted to make a change in his life. Or maybe he just saw the opportunities and the fresh start that a life in the ashram could afford him. Of course, spiritual benefits were immeasurable, but there was more to it than that. Temple folk always had amazing, delectable vegetarian meals and a roof over their head in charming ashrams, often surrounded by beautiful, well kept temple grounds. They were also offered numerous opportunities to travel the country, even the planet, on preaching missions. It wasn't a bad life for someone who, not too long ago, was on a boat fleeing a communist regime.

Moreover, Alan told tall tales. I believed the boat story, because Alejandro had confirmed it, but Alan also said that he was once wrongfully accused of robbing a bank, and later acquitted. He was currently countersuing the City of Miami for half a million dollars, and if he won, he wanted to use it to start a Krishna conscious orphanage so he could fulfill his dream of looking after children.

I raised an eyebrow, remembering his peculiar Facebook friend list.

*

Once the Sunday program had started, surrounded by the other women in the temple, I danced and danced to the booming kirtan. The trio stayed on the other side, dancing with the men. After the Hare Krishna mantra, we sat on the floor around the main singer as he sang a *bhajan*, while some people played musical instruments such as *kartals* and *mridangas* (Indian drums).

We sang a beautiful Bengali song glorifying Radha and Krishna. It was my first time hearing the song, but I would never forget it:

Jaya Radhe, jaya Krishna, jaya Vrindavan,
Sri Govinda, Gopinatha, Madana mohan,

Shyama kunda, Radha kunda, Giri Govardhan,
Kalindi Jamuna jaya, jaya Mahavan!

After singing and dancing, there was a short lecture. I couldn't hear much because the acoustics in the temple weren't very good. I tapped the shoulder of a young woman in front of me. She was wearing a sari and had brown skin, but once I asked her what the speaker was talking about, it was clear she wasn't Indian.

She shook her head. "Don't know English," she told me, in a thick Spanish accent. "You know?"

"Yes, but I can't hear him."

*

The temple had an anti-food wasting policy. Vegetarian food cooked while thinking of Krishna and offered to the deity of Lord Krishna—food which Krishna himself had eaten—was blessed and not to be discarded. But after I made a generous donation for the meal, the servers tended to lay it on thick. There was no way I could have fit all of that food into my stomach.

"Un momento," I told the trio, excusing myself to use the bathroom.

In the dank powder room, I stared at myself in the mirror. There was barely any soap left. I pulled my belly top down awkwardly. I was feeling nervous.

I was sitting with the trio as the center of attention. I hated being the center of attention, and worse, I wasn't used to it. I couldn't eat while being watched and interrogated like that.

"Everything okay?" asked Alan.

"Yeah...coming."

I flushed the toilet and turned the sink on and off.

"Thought you died in there!" said Alan. "Oh hey, while you were gone...Alejandro said next time you come to Miami, you can stay at his place. No need to get a hotel. Or you can have a room in the temple, in exchange for volunteering. When are you coming back?"

It appeared I wasn't going to get a break that easily. I had to just embrace the moment and soak up the sun.

"Did you like the program today?" Jose asked me, before he giddily gulped down a cup of the blessed caranamrita, the milk and honey mixture used to bathe deities of the Lord.

"Yes. I couldn't hear the lecture, but I love to dance."

"I saw that!" affirmed Alan. "You looked like you might go into ecstasy any moment. Did you like the song?"

"Of course. It's a Bengali song."

"You speak Bengali?"

"My dad is Bengali."

"Teach us! Teach us!" demanded Jose.

"Is he alright?"

"He had too much...*honey*."

"Well, it's not too different from Spanish. Take the Spanish word for soap, *jabón*. In Bengali, it's *shobon*. The word for dream is *sueño*, in Bengali, it's *shopno*."

Alan and Jose seemed to "ooh" and "aah" at whatever I said, while Alejandro just gave me ambiguous glances beneath long, dark eyelashes.

A young boy made his way around the temple, handing out tiny bottles of honey that the temple had cultivated.

"How do you say *miel* in Bengali?"

"Madhu."

Becoming a polyglot was a long-held dream of mine, but until Livemocha.com, I had always been unilingual. I had beat a decent amount of Spanish into my brain, but not quite enough to call myself fluent—especially since words seemed to evade me when I felt nervous or put on the spot.

Being able to find the interconnectedness of various languages was actually to my detriment. I would mix Spanish with my high school French, and when I went to India with my dad, I switched Bengali words for Spanish ones without noticing. I thought that if I practiced French more and gained a better understanding of the language, it would help to separate it from other languages in my mind. With that rationale, I took French lessons on Livemocha.com, but kept speaking or writing Spanish in all my practice assignments.

It was getting later and later, and I dreaded taking the bus with only the giggly, silly Jose for companionship. I was relieved when Alan announced that Alejandro could drive Jose and I home—a drastic change from hours before, when I had dreaded getting into a car with these men! I now saw that they would do me no harm. I still didn't trust Alan one iota, but I had somewhat figured him out.

"You can throw away the food if you can't finish it," Alan told me.

I appreciated his comment. I had been teased in other temples for not being able to finish dinner. Wasting food was considered a sin.

"Thanks, but I think I'll take it with me. It will be a nice change from pancakes...as long as no one else steals it."

I took the plate and my cup of the blessed mixture of caranamrita.

We stood to leave.

"Oh, don't forget your honey!" I said to Alejandro. I passed the bottle to him at the same time as he reached for it, and our hands touched momentarily. I felt a sensation I hadn't felt since I was a teenager.

He looked me in the eyes for the first time, and it was electric.

*

"We'll chat on Skype and Facebook, okay?" asked Alan.

"Sure."

We were parked in front of the hostel, but none of them seemed to want to let me go.

"Can we drop you off at the airport tomorrow?"

"No thanks...I'm leaving early in the morning."

It was partly true. My flight wasn't until the afternoon, but I planned to pack and leave early. Relinquishing control over something so important, like my return trip to my old life, wasn't something I was comfortable with.

"Maybe I'll give you a call or send you a message if I ever go to Canada."

"Okay."

"And you'll let us know if you come to Miami?"

"Sure I will."

"Oh. Okay. Well, come back soon."

"I'll see. It was nice to meet you all!"

"My pleasure," said Alan.

There was only one of them that I really, truly hoped I'd see again. But I was almost certain I never would.

Returning

I walked back into my hostel. It was past nine p.m., and now that I was left to my own devices, my appetite had returned. I decided to warm up my dinner in the kitchen microwave, and return my "weapon."

My day was coming to an end, while everyone else in the city was just starting to come alive. The kitchen table was packed with inebriated young women, clinging wildly to the arms of foreign young men.

"Oh WOW. That smells AMAZING," an early twenty-something said to me, eyeing my plate from the moment I walked in. She was just a *little* too close for comfort, and spoke just a *little* too loudly.

"Not too long in the microwave, sweetie. DON'T get cancer. I don't like cancer!" she slurred, pointing a finger at me warningly.

I clandestinely slipped the—almost empty—soap squirter back by the sink, and left the kitchen.

How did it get so empty?

I opened my purse to find that the inside was dripping wet. Miraculously, my *Gita* was still intact, which was all that really mattered.

Against house rules, I went up to my room to eat. On the way there, I saw the Irani intern from days ago, sitting on the couch with her laptop. She was sharing her earbuds with my German roommate, indulging her in a Bollywood romance.

"Hi," I said to the Irani intern. "Do you want to try this drink?"

I passed her the cup of caranamrita.

"Sure."

She snatched it from me and swallowed it down, unquestioning. "Oh, God!" she said, wincing.

That which in the beginning may be just like poison but at the end is just like nectar and which awakens one to self-realization is said to be happiness in the mode of goodness.

—The Bhagavad Gita, 18.37

"That's a taste of *real* Indian culture," I said, smiling.

She forcefully passed me the empty cup. "Yep. Typical Indian. Much too sweet!"

I tilted my head. "You're welcome."

"Where did you get this?"

"The temple."

The Irani girl gave me a Mona Lisa smile. "You found a temple around here? Impressive."

"A temple?" asked my roommate, removing an earbud. "That's an interesting thing to do. Is it near the beach?"

"No, you have to take the Metromover. By the way, this is my last night. I'll leave the toothpaste out for you tomorrow morning."

"Danke!"

"Auf wiedersehen!"

She smiled.

*

I woke up at the crack of dawn to see the ocean one last time. The pink sun was just beginning to rise, and the sight was splendid.

Unlike the first time I set a bare foot on South Beach, this time there was no one else around me. No beach volleyball players. No lovers kissing in the water. No pick-up artists sharing beers, looking for their next target to approach.

There was only the girl I had seen before, reading her German book.

"Hi! Will you take my picture?" she asked me.

"Of course."

I took one of her with her camera, and then one of the ocean, sun, and sand with mine. Like so many times before, my photography skills were severely inadequate for capturing the raw beauty of nature, God's creation, in that moment.

If hundreds of thousands of suns were to rise at once into the sky, their radiance might resemble the effulgence of the Supreme Person in that universal form.

—The Bhagavad Gita, 11.12

I looked down at my hands and saw the remnants of my DIY Dior manicure from the beginning of my long journey. It seemed like eons ago that I had so shamelessly indulged myself with that tiny sample bottle at the Sephora near Times Square. I rose and went for a long dip in the ocean. I scratched at my nails wildly under the water, removing the manicure's last traces. With the great hebetude that comes from spending far too much time on the beach, I lay flat, floating in the star position, allowing myself to get just a little more burned.

I felt like I was at a dead end in life, so I took a much needed, spiritually infused vacation, in which I had made it all the way to

187

the southernmost end of the United States. There was nowhere else I needed to be. It was time to head home.

*

Taking the Metromover for the final time was no less exciting than the first time I had ever been on it. I hadn't travelled all that much in my life, and I had only been on an airplane a handful of times, but my ride to the Miami International Airport was by far the most scenic trip to an airport I had ever taken. I got one final tour of the town before departing, most likely never to return.

I had travelled before, but this was my first real *vacation*. The first time I had ever wandered for the sake of wandering. I wasn't visiting family or getting a course credit. I was just being in the moment, absorbing whatever I could about where I was.

I had the chance to experience America. I loved the way that each state felt like a different country. I enjoyed trying all the ice cream truck flavours in New York. I loved the kindness of strangers in Washington, and the hospitality of the Deep South. I savoured soaking up the sun while I lay on my back and drifted in the ocean, finally reaching my journey's end.

I went through security smoothly and got a seat at the gate well before departure. I retrieved my journal from my purse and wrote down my final reflections and experiences while I waited.

Someone was calling me. I shuffled through my bag for my cell phone and didn't recognize the number on the display. I answered anyway.

"Samita speaking."

"Hello, is this Samita?"

I hated when people did that.

"Yes, this is she."

"It's Glenn from the employment agency. We found an opening for you. Did you get our email?"

"Maybe. I've been travelling, so I haven't had much time to check emails."

"Can you do an interview later today? It's for a writing position."

"Oh? What kind of writing position?"

"It's office writing. Namely data entry."

"I'm sorry. I'm not interested. Thank you for thinking of me."

I knew that it was time to stop pushing.

I had been thinking about becoming a business owner for some time, but I didn't have the confidence to pursue it. My parents encouraged the idea, and I had scoffed at them irritably. I wanted the job security that a nine-to-five would provide me. But now I could see that security, both in the office world and beyond, was a myth. You could do everything right, but nothing would come to you if it wasn't Krishna's will.

*

The airplane flew over Miami Beach, giving me a peak at the deep blue, endless, unknowable ocean that represents all that is awesome and incomprehensible about Lord Krishna.

Having the aisle seat, I reached over my seatmate and opened the window, craning my neck to behold the beauty.

"Hey—that's my window!" he peevishly asserted.

We had both paid for a plane ticket on a commercial airline, but I shrugged off the comment. Once we were off in the air, passing through the Deep South and Washington D.C. within hours—places that had taken me days to cover on land—I reached over and shut the window, earning his ire in order to get some shelter from the blazing sun. When we were about to land at our stopover in New York City, I asked the man to open the window again for me, so I could get some killer airplane shots of the famous city.

He sighed loudly. "Oh for fuck's sake! Tourist..." he grumbled acrimoniously.

"Thank you!" I responded sweetly, reaching my camera over him to take the shots unabashedly.

He was clearly suffering, but I did not return his rancor.

*

From anger, complete delusion arises, and from delusion bewilderment of memory. When memory is bewildered, intelligence is lost, and when intelligence is lost one falls down again into the material pool.

There are three gates leading to this hell—lust, anger and greed. Every sane man should give these up.

—The Bhagavad Gita, 2.63, 16.21

Although side-by-side with me, my seatmate did not see what I saw when I looked down at our marvelous planet. I hoped one day, he would. The truth is concrete and unsubjective, but happiness is a state of mind.

We landed, and I, along with a few other passengers, clapped for the pilot while my seatmate gave me an inimical look as if to question my sanity. He hurried ahead of me off the plane, an ephemeral character gone from the story of my life as quickly as he had entered. New York City was his final destination.

I went along to line up at the final gate, catching my connection to Pearson International Airport. On the way, I walked by a large wall advertisement. It read, "From the center of the world to the rest of it." I wondered whether or not it was tongue-in-cheek.

I got to my gate just as we were already about to board, and people had already begun to line up. I joined the back of the line, went up in the air once more, and descended in what felt like a millisecond.

Travelling by "airbus" gives us the illusion that the world is so much smaller than it is in actuality. You don't get the flavour of each State, or town you pass. You miss the small pleasures of sandwiches at roadside pit stops and conversations with (mostly) friendly, albeit temporary travel companions. Gliding through the stratosphere wasn't my favourite way to travel, but when time was of the essence—rather, when the destination took priority over the journey—it was the way to go.

*

When I arrived back in Canada after almost a month of fulfilling my wanderlust, several things changed for me, both big and small.

I never liked people knowing things I don't know. That's why I taught myself Spanish, and that's why, even though I never intended to work in a laboratory, I found myself enrolled in a BSc program at the rigorous Athabasca University just three months after my return. Some people sneered when I announced it, telling me that I'd never use the information I learned, but they were wrong. The scientific knowledge I gained was profoundly useful in academic and technical editing gigs, as well as in my own writing.

I also bought my first car. Cars are practically a necessity for anyone living in suburban North America. I had wanted one since high school, but I always put it off. I told myself that someone in my position didn't need a car. I told myself I'd get one when I graduated from university. I told myself I'd buy one when I got a job (although I was asked countless times during interviews if I already had a car). Deep down, I just didn't feel deserving. But I was finished with waiting around for life to happen to me.

In the same train of thought, I launched my business. I knew that it was time to embrace what my parents, and Krishna, had been trying to tell me for so long.

Most other business owners I've talked to said they felt compelled to start their own businesses. Office life wasn't for them. They hated the corporate world. They wanted more for themselves. They had a message they wanted to share.

There are so many successful entrepreneurs who I truly respect, and they swear that they are in control of their own destiny. They are marketing geniuses that have given me valuable guidance in material matters, but in this regard, they are clueless.

I didn't choose my path. Krishna chose it for me. I am not in control; Krishna is. He is the one who wanted more for me. This is what I say when people ask me why I chose to start a business: I didn't. This is also what I say when people ask me why I choose to stand up for animals: don't ask me! I had no control over my destiny, and anyone who thinks they do is deeply delusional.

This isn't a bad thing. This is a beautiful thing. I want to thank the Supreme Lord, my friend and well-wisher Lord Krishna for blessing me so abundantly.

I'm not special. I'm not "chosen." God cares about the immortal soul in each and every person, plant, and animal equally, and with His divine will, He arranges our experiences perfectly so that we learn what we need to learn before we can go back to Him, never to return.

Oh, and I finally got my glasses fixed.

Always think of Me, become My devotee, worship Me and offer your homage unto Me. Thus you will come to Me without fail. I promise you this because you are My very dear friend.

Abandon all varieties of religion and just surrender unto Me. I shall deliver you from all sinful reactions. Do not fear.

—The Bhagavad Gita, 18.65, 18.66

WHAT HAPPENED TO MY TRAVEL COMPANIONS

Keshav graduated and got an environmental science position, where he works in species conservation.

Drew left the South for the Golden State, where he started his own design company.

Rasa is still living in Europe, but she did manage to leave Lithuania. She now resides in Germany, where she is still searching for her dark prince.

Jeanie found true love. She actually got married before her younger sister, and now has a baby with her handsome new hubby.

Charlie continues trotting the globe and has taken a few more stabs at entrepreneurialism, for as long as he is able to stick with one idea or country. I ran into him again months later in a temple in Canada. When we met once more and reminisced about our beachside days in Miami, he asked me if I remembered "that arrogant bugger" from the hostel lobby. I told him it was well past time to let it go.

Finally, I was wrong in my assumption that I'd never see Alejandro again.

ABOUT THE AUTHOR

Samita Sarkar is a full-time writer, editor, and animal advocate. She lives in Canada.

www.ingramcontent.com/pod-product-compliance
Lightning Source LLC
Chambersburg PA
CBHW060206070426
42447CB00035B/2748